"The Road to Sweet Success is an absolt
us all that anything is possible. Janette
unlikely story of overcoming all odds to
Her insights will guide and inspire anyone ~~ ~~~~~~~ ~~~ ~~ ~~~~~~
to start with a dream, no matter how improbable."

~ **Hal G. Halladay**, Chief People Officer, Infusionsoft

"Janette always strikes me as a deeply joyful person. She manages her healthy family and her booming business with good humor and fun, and she's always ready to help a friend. She's the Boss that everyone secretly has a crush on, the Best Friend you can have a margarita with and the Brilliant Marketer who knows how to communicate with clarity and authenticity."

~ **Samantha Bennett**, The Organized Artist Company and Best-selling Author, "Get It Done: From Procrastination to Creative Genius in 15 Minutes a Day"

"Janette is a role model for so many people. Her life-changing transformation has given her greater fulfillment and purpose in life; she's living her dream. Today, she strives to empower others to fulfill their own dreams and live the lifestyle they've always wanted."

~ **Trish McCarty**, Founder and President, StarShine Academy

"Janette is a trusted mentor and friend, who has provided invaluable expertise in building business systems and offering counsel for my businesses. She has always exceeded my expectations when assessing and responding to my needs. With her input at monthly CEO Mastermind gatherings, she has added an expert perspective that gave me tools to overcome obstacles that my mind saw as roadblocks."

~ **Edward Maznio**, President, Office Guardian

"I have had the opportunity to work with Janette in various ways over the past few years as a finalist in Infusionsoft's Ultimate Marketer competition and when she came out on top during our global partner competition, generating the most Infusionsoft sales. Although Janette has won many awards and accolades, what I find most impressive about her is the way she is impacting the world as a business leader, advocate for women and active member of her community."

~ **Cindy Eagar**, Director of Elite Programs, Infusionsoft

"The two things I admire most about Janette are: 1) her commitment to setting and achieving goals and 2) her commitment to her family. Janette's passion for these two things is contagious. I have witnessed time and again the way she inspires people whether she is speaking from the stage or working one-on-one with someone. We should all aspire to dream big like Janette does!"

~ **Jessica Maes**, Owner, Maes Consulting Group

"Janette personifies the statement - if you can see it, you can achieve it. By demonstrating her ability to set a goal (i.e. win Infusionsoft Ultimate Marketer of Year Award) and achieve it with a well laid out plan, Janette has become an inspiration to me. Through working with her, I now know I have the ability and confidence to achieve my goals through visioning and a well laid out plan."

~ **Rich Rose**, President, Strategic Solutions Group, Inc.

"My fondest memory of Janette during The Big Drive was that she knew she was going to win this contest from day one. There were other participants with more experience and more reputation but it never seemed to faze Janette. She stayed calm, focused and determined to win this contest. Even as we approached the end of the contest, she never seemed stressed or worried. She continued to do the work and, in the end, won the big prize."

~ **Dave Sherman**, Marketing and Networking Specialist, Dave Sherman Speaks

"Success is difficult to achieve when you have no destination or goal. Janette helped me to focus on what it is I want to achieve in the next five years. She's helped me to visualize what it will feel like to reach My Audacious Goals. I'm excited to wake up and go to work everyday because it's clear to me WHY."

~ **Jerry Levinson**, Owner, Carpets of Arizona

"It has been a privilege to interact with Janette Gleason in our CEO Mastermind Group. The before and after results she gets for her clients are absolutely amazing, as was her personal transformation."

~ **Chuck Trautman**, CEO, Arizona Marketing Association

"Janette is a truly unique and inspiring individual. Yes, she's charming, fun, and capable, but she's also a driven and ambitious woman with keen business savvy. Her ability to balance running a successful small business without compromising her commitment to her family is a shining example that entrepreneurship doesn't have to cripple you. As I start and build my own company, I'm motivated by what I know to be possible because talented people like Janette are blazing the trail."

~ **Greg Jenkins**, Founder, Monkeypod Marketing

"Working with Janette is a great experience! She has a tremendous ability to help others set goals, visualize, organize a success plan, and then consistently work that plan to achieve the goals. As things progress on that path, she is a positive, steady influence who knows what it takes to succeed. And perhaps best of all, she is kind, empathetic, and truly cares about others. I have found her to truly be an example of achieving success without compromising values."

~ **Clint Johnson**, Founder, Profitable PPOs

"Janette's coaching, consulting, and teaching methods aren't from theory but rather from her experience as a business owner. These are practices she's implemented not only for our businesses, but also for her clients with great success. I'm proud to get to see her genius being shared with the world so that others may enjoy the road to sweet success, too."

~ **Joe Gleason**, CEO, Gleason Financial Group, LLC

The ROAD to
Sweet Success

ENJOY THE RIDE TOWARD CRUSHING YOUR GOALS

JANETTE GLEASON

The ROAD *to* Sweet Success
ENJOY THE RIDE TOWARD CRUSHING YOUR GOALS

www.JanetteGleason.com

Cover design and layout by Hollister Design Group
Photography by Darby Simon

Published by Gleason Consulting Group, LLC

ISBN #978-0-9893147-1-8

Dedication

I dedicate this book to my children, Joey, Jianna, and Jillian.

It is my greatest pride to be your mother and to watch you learn, grow, and share your gifts with those around you. I'm so thankful for the light you shine on the world and the joy you bring me each and every day. I write this book to serve as a guidebook for you. I commit to always encourage you to pursue your true heart's desires, and I hold these wishes for you:

~ *May you achieve your goals and live your dreams.*

~ *May you create the life you desire.*

~ *May you live in abundance and in constant gratitude.*

~ *May you experience success in all your endeavors.*

~ *May you learn and grow from the obstacles you encounter.*

~ *May your recognize the seeds of growth and knowledge that result from your failures.*

~ *May you remember to take time to reflect, rest, and rejuvenate.*

~ *May you enjoy every step along the road to your sweet success.*

… And may ALL your dreams true!

Table of Contents

Table of Contents

Introduction

Are you feeling frustrated with yourself and the life you're living? Did you set some goals, make a vision board, even get started toward those goals, but after a while found that you didn't achieve what you set out to accomplish? Maybe you're feeling a little unfulfilled? There are unfinished projects you've been working on for years, but you have no time to complete them with all the other responsibilities you have in your life. Are you feeling anxious as you're watching the time tick by, because the dreams on your bucket list remain unachieved for you? Maybe you're feeling a little stuck, like you're not attracting the right opportunities, experiences, and people into your life.

Take a few moments to imagine how your life will change by actually achieving your goals. Are you going to have more peace of mind and security from earning that extra income? Will you have a blast taking that dream vacation with your family? Will you feel extreme pride as you receive recognition for a job well done? Can you just imagine the pure excitement you will feel when you receive a promotion at work and step into your new role? Think about the fulfillment you will feel when you complete that big project, move into your new home, or start that new business.

By achieving that next level of success, you will feel a new sense of accomplishment. You will show yourself that you've got what it takes to do whatever you set your mind to. Achieving your big, hairy, audacious goals will help you feel more fulfilled and give you a renewed sense of purpose. You'll jump out of bed in the morning with a spring in your step as you move closer toward your goals each and every day.

THE GOAL-DRIVEN LIFE

I've always been a goal-oriented, goal-driven person. From winning organ contests as a child, to graduating Magna Cum Laude in college, to starting my own business, to becoming a best-selling author, I've lived life as an achiever, a person who thrives on setting a goal and reaching it. My determination and extreme focus have served me well throughout the years. Because I've put myself out there and pushed myself to achieve high levels of success, I've experienced the pride of a job well done, traveled the world, and realized many of my dreams. Being recognized as Teacher of the Year, studying in Ecuador for a summer, walking the red carpet in Hollywood, and holding my first book in my hands are just some of the greatest moments of my life. Because, you see, these were all things I purposefully set out to accomplish, even if they sometimes seemed nearly impossible from the start.

However, because I've pushed myself over the years, I have also fallen flat on my face, many, many times. I've been rejected and failed miserably. I've had disappointments and heartbreak countless times. I didn't get selected as a member of the varsity dance team in high school. I've been passed up for what I thought would be my dream job. I've come in as runner-up, time and time again, wishing so badly that one day I would finally hold that first place trophy. I've even gone through a foreclosure, losing our home and holding my head down in shame and embarrassment. But, I've always learned something about myself from each of those experiences. My failures and disappointments have revealed some valuable lessons: the weaknesses I needed to overcome. Each of these painful experiences carried with it the seeds of growth and an opportunity to transform.

In recent years, I've become a diligent student of the idea that we can create the life or the experiences we choose. I've learned that my mindset, thoughts, and actions contribute to that which I'm experiencing around me. I've followed and studied with some of the top thought leaders in this space, like Jack Canfield, Brian Tracy, Sonia Choquette, and the late Wayne Dyer. I read about developing the right mindset to achieve your goals, how the law of attraction can be used to bring you what you desire, and how to follow proven success principles that will help you realize your dreams. I began to apply these principles, tools, and strategies in my life. Could I, in a more consistent way, achieve my goals? Could I stop falling flat on my face or being a runner-up? I hired coaches, read books, attended conferences, and sought out mentors to help me figure this all out. With varying degrees of success, I realized there was something to this, but not always 100% of the time for me.

My logical, methodical brain wanted to conduct an experi-ment, in a very scientific way. I needed to choose something big, something nearly impossible in my mind's eye for me to achieve. Will these principles in fact work if I apply them consistently and intentionally? I needed to pick something so grandiose and so colossal to convince me. That's when I saw the announcement of The Big Drive contest. As a certified consultant and reseller with Infusionsoft, a sales and marketing automation software program for small businesses, I had the opportunity to enter a sales competition. The person who sold the most software subscriptions in a three-month period would win the grand prize: a brand-new Chevrolet Camaro. I thought, "That's it! Perfect, I'm going after the car!" The possibility of me winning was such a far stretch. I had tough competition and completely lacked this type of sales experience. When I realized I faced the impossible, that's when I knew it was the perfect destination of choice.

The contest was, well, an exhilarating ride! A thrilling series of events from ups and downs, to bumps in the road, to magical moments, and sometimes, through painful, yet beautiful metamorphoses. Step by step and inch by inch, I achieved small wins during those three months that led to my ultimate victory. I got focused, developed a support network, and retrained my brain to think like a winner. I overcame obstacles, worked on my weaknesses, and used my skills and talents in my favor. It was a neck-and-neck, nail biter of a race, but I crossed the finish line as the grand champion and won that Camaro! That beautiful car sits in my garage today as a glorious representation of true success. It's the proof that I needed in order to know whole-heartedly that you **can** create and, even more importantly, that you **do** create everything in your life. But, more of that story to come...

THE JOURNEY CONTINUES

Crossing that finish line wasn't the end of my journey. People were really curious to learn how I won the car. To their surprise, it wasn't **all** about hard work or even pure luck. I began to share with them the techniques, tools, and strategies I used during the contest. I explained how I created a thermometer poster to track my sales, sent positive email messages to myself each day, visualized giving my acceptance speech each night before falling asleep, and much, much more. Then, people began to approach me to coach them to achieve their big, hairy, audacious goals, too.

Through my coaching, events, and programs, my clients are using the same principles to achieve great accomplishments. From winning contests, to getting promotions, to leveling up their businesses, to crushing company goals, and more, my clients are experiencing transformations and achieving successes beyond their wildest dreams. And to my great delight, it's been my privilege and honor to guide them and to share in their experiences of success. What an incredible gift!

That's why I decided to write this book, to share with you how I won my prized Camaro, to teach you the principles that have worked for me and that now help my clients achieve the next level of success. My wish is to guide you to implementing strategies that will move you closer to your goals, to inspire you to go after your biggest dreams, and to empower you to live a lifestyle that brings you joy and abundance.

This book serves as a map that guides you to your success and helps you:

- Get really focused and committed to your goals.
- Learn a step-by-step process to achieving success.
- Equip yourself with simple tools and strategies.
- Create new habits of success.
- Develop a support network that will cheer for you and guide you throughout this process.

This book will also help you realize that you are already successful. Throughout your life you have accomplished some amazing things, and I will help you use those experiences to your advantage. You are constantly creating, whether you realize it or not! You've had success in your life, and you've probably had some failures, too. But, you have a drive to achieve more, to do something bigger than you've ever done, and now it's your turn to claim your spot once again in the driver's seat.

The order of the chapters is designed to build upon the concepts you will learn in the previous chapters. For maximum results, I suggest going through them in order the first time you read the book. Then, you can go back to specific areas of need or topics you wish to revisit down the road.

Each chapter contains:

The Big Drive Stories: I begin every chapter sharing stories and anecdotes from my experiences during The Big Drive sales contest. I had my sights set on winning the grand prize, that brand-new Camaro, and succeeded. This contest was a transformational experience for me, one where I tested all of the principles outlined in this book. These stories will introduce you to each principle, along with the tools and strategies I implemented during the contest.

Tools and Strategies: In the main chapter sections, we'll get specific about applying each of the principles as I describe the nuts and bolts, the helpful tools and strategies that you can pick and choose from to practice using in your life. Then, I'll tie in some of my clients' stories of how they use these strategies and other personal examples, so you can really see how those tools, these nuts and bolts, can be applied in **your** daily life.

Get Into Gear: This section will summarize the main learning points and ideas covered in the chapter. These highlights will help you stay focused and remember key ideas. It will be a handy point of reference for you while you begin to practice applying the techniques from that chapter.

Accelerate Toward Your Success: You'll also find action items you can complete to accelerate toward your goals. These simple activities will guide you in putting the tools and strategies you read about into practice. You'll begin to see yourself moving closer to your goals with the completion of each activity.

On the Road Reflections: At the end of the chapter, you'll be given ideas for journaling, so you can write and reflect throughout the process. You will be provided with questions or prompts to record your thoughts, experiences, and ideas. Pen to paper writing is a wonderful habit that will enhance your journey to success.

POSITIONING YOURSELF FOR SUCCESS

As you get ready for the journey to begin, you'll want to secure your pole position, the most favorable place to be at the start of the race. You can position yourself for success by keeping the following tips in mind:

1. **Have an open mind and an open heart.** Be receptive to new and different ideas. While you review and begin to practice the concepts in this book, be true to your own feelings. Be completely honest and candid with yourself to start off on the right track toward achieving your goals. You deserve to experience the joy and success that you truly desire, so approach your journey with an open mind and an open heart.

2. **Be willing to try something new or different.** This book will push you out of your comfort zone from time to time and will encourage you to be diligent about creating new habits. You will be prompted to integrate various strategies in your daily life by writing, playing games, and getting crafty. Trust me, it'll be fun! Be willing to try something new. If you want different results in your life, you need to be willing and able to try something new.

3. **Get focused.** Each week, take the time to stay on course. Learn the content, embrace these principles, and apply them to your daily life. Direct your attention and efforts to the ideas and strategies presented to you. Each chapter will help you build the skills required to get to the next level, and taking focused action will be crucial to your success.

4. **Involve others in the process.** Find someone who also wants to achieve something big and work through this book together. Maybe it's your spouse, a friend, a close family member, or a partner. A great way to learn is by teaching someone else the concepts you are studying. Anchor your learning by talking about your progress and sharing your successes with someone you trust.

5. **Show up to your goals each and every day.** You have the desire to change, and you want to experience the joy of living out your dreams. It's important for you to show up to

your goals every day. Even a small action can have a big impact on your success. Make your happiness and success a priority and commit to taking action on a daily basis.

I know you have big dreams and the desire to achieve something incredible. Are you ready to get to the next level, either in your business or in your personal life? This book will help get you there. It's time to make some changes in your life, get clear about where you're headed, and give it your all! By applying the principles in this book, you'll experience a transformation. It will be a transformation that gives you the skills and confidence to **always** go after your dreams, no matter how big or small. Your success is just around the corner, so buckle up and get ready for the ride of your life!

Let the journey toward your sweet success begin...

CHAPTER

> "All our dreams can come true if we have the courage to pursue them."
>
> ~ Walt Disney

I t all comes down to this moment — the start of the race! You have a great desire to live your dreams and achieve your goals. Excitement is building as the drivers enter the track. The fans started showing up hours ago, excited to cheer you on during this amazing race. Your vehicle is waiting for you on the track. As you step into the car and sit in the driver's seat, you look out ahead of you. You are ready to embark on your new adventure, and you can feel the pure adrenaline rushing throughout your body. As you begin to bring your destination into clearer focus, your imagination is running wild and your enthusiasm is hard to contain. You might know exactly where you are headed, or maybe you need a little guidance in mapping your route. It's time to get clear on your destination as you enter the road to your sweet success and prepare to begin your journey. Now, let's fire up your engine. It's going to be an exhilarating ride!

PULLING UP TO THE STARTING LINE

A few years back, my job title was "stay-at-home mom." I was living my dream of being home with our three small children. I loved my role as a young mother. I enjoyed the precious moments of caring for our babies and watching them grow into toddlers. I had taken a step back from my career as an elementary school teacher to stay home with the kids. I still had my foot in the working world, playing a minor supportive role in my husband's financial planning business where I helped with payroll and higher-level planning.

Right before Thanksgiving 2010, Joe's office manager quit suddenly. I stepped in to help Joe at the office until we could hire and train somebody new. While my mom and dad watched the kids for me, I went into the office for a few hours each day to keep things going. I sorted through the mail, answered the phones, and greeted clients. During quiet moments, I started tinkering around with Infusionsoft, the sales and marketing automation software Joe's team had been using for a couple of years, and discovered we had a powerful tool in our hands. Soon, we hired a couple of new employees, and I helped get them up and running quickly. Then, I happily headed back home to our children, but didn't completely hand in my most recent job title — Marketing Specialist — quite yet.

I continued helping Joe and his staff from the comfort of my own home. After watching tutorials and training webinars about Infusionsoft's features, I saw how powerful the software could be for a small business owner. I learned about marketing and how implementing life cycle marketing strategies could help our business grow. Over the period of a few weeks, I fell in love with the software and with marketing automation! All of a sudden, I found myself in a new career having the best of both worlds by staying home with the kids and working at the same time.

After just a short time, I implemented what I had learned about marketing and developed a new campaign that doubled our revenue during tax season. Shortly thereafter, Infusionsoft announced its annual Ultimate Marketer Contest to recognize top customers who had experienced results directly from the use of the software. I thought, "Why not? I'm going to submit my entry and see what happens!" I really had no idea what I was getting myself into at that point. To my great delight, I was selected as one of the top three finalists out of hundreds of applications. A few months later I found myself at Infusionsoft's annual user conference speaking in front of 1,000 people to share my success story.

However, I did not walk away with the title of Ultimate Marketer that year. I came in as the runner-up. Finding myself in this spot once again left me completely and utterly devastated. I was so embarrassed and felt like a failure. It took me some time to get over it, but when I did, I realized that by being a finalist I WAS in fact a winner. The recognition from that contest helped launch my own consulting business to help other small business owners with their sales and marketing automation. Through the start-up process, I became an Infusionsoft Certified Partner and quickly began building my clientele list.

Fast-forward to the spring of 2013, Infusionsoft invited me to its partner banquet and awards ceremony during its annual conference. I remember sitting at the table with my husband and a few colleagues, and after dinner, Infusionsoft began handing out awards to recognize the top sales people - those who had sold the most Infusionsoft subscriptions that year. I saw all of these men going up on stage, receiving their awards, and it really lit a fire under me. I got so excited about wanting to join in on the game and imagined being up on that stage the next year to be recognized for MY achievements. That was a defining moment for me. I felt a great desire to go after this new goal.

A couple months later, there was an announcement from Infusionsoft about a contest called The Big Drive. The person who sold the most software subscriptions during the period from Memorial Day to Labor Day would win a brand-new Chevrolet Camaro. The timing was perfect. I had that fire lit inside of me and the desire and ambition to go for it. In years past, I wasn't much of a salesperson. During my entire career, I had sold only a handful of Infusionsoft subscriptions. I had been much more focused on helping and servicing existing customers to maximize their use of the software in their businesses. I tried to throw my hat in the ring for prior Infusionsoft sales contests and incentives, but the competition always smoked me right out of the gates. This time around, I had my mind set on winning the grand prize, and for some reason I felt that this was my chance to be number one.

I made the declaration that I was going to win that Camaro. I remember repeatedly saying to my friends, family, and business associates, "Mark my words, that car is mine." Sometimes I could see the doubt in their eyes as they gave me a token nod or a pat on the back, but it didn't faze me. To me, there was no doubt in my mind that the Camaro **was** mine. I didn't know HOW I was going to win and accomplish this big, hairy, audacious goal, but I knew exactly WHAT I wanted and WHY I wanted it. I wanted to have that car more than anything else and to finally be number one for the first time in my life. I wanted to show myself that I could do it. Because if I did, I knew I could accomplish anything I set out to do. I was in the driver's seat, had pulled up to the starting line, and revved my engine. I could feel that this was going to be a thrilling race to the finish line!

IT ALL STARTS WITH A DREAM

What does your heart desire? It's time for you to open your eyes to all of the possibilities and to start dreaming again. As a child, you might have had thoughts about what you desired for your life. What did you want to be when you grew up? What places did you want to travel to or visit? What did you want to accomplish? You had all sorts of visions and desires that would catch your imagination. As you got older, maybe life just kind of happened and people or circumstances crushed your dreams. Maybe your failures caused you to become discouraged along the way, and you gave up on your dreams. Now is the time to get back to that childlike state of wonder where you are dreaming of and wishing for the life experiences that will make you hop out of bed every morning with a spring in your step and a zest for life.

"The starting point of all achievement is desire."

~ Napoleon Hill

Your Bucket List

A good place to start dreaming is by creating your "Bucket List." Grab a sheet of paper and let your imagination run wild. What are the things that you want to accomplish before you kick the bucket? We know that life is precious and that our time is limited here on this Earth, so why wait 10, 20, or 30 years to start living out those wishes and desires you hold in your heart?

A couple of months ago, I cleaned out a dresser drawer and came across an old notebook that I had used as a journal. As I flipped through the pages, I discovered a short bucket list of things I really wanted to do in my lifetime. To my great delight, three of the items on my list had been accomplished. "Travel to Italy" was top on my list! In 2013, my husband and I were on a cruise to the French Riviera and made a couple of stops in Italy: Portofino and Santa Margherita. I grabbed a pen and crossed that item off of the list. Check! Another item listed in my journal was to contact and meet my birth mother. I was given up for adoption as a baby, and I was able to reconnect with her and get answers about how I came into this world! Check! It felt so good to cross that off of my list too! The third item was taking our kids to Disneyland. For three years in a row, we visited the "Happiest Place on Earth," rode Space Mountain countless times, ate Mickey Mouse shaped beignets at New Orleans Square, and made some incredible memories with our family. Check! A third item was crossed off and a smile was plastered on my face that day as I reminisced about these amazing accomplishments.

Now, not everything has been checked off my list yet. I still want to go to Chichén Itzá and climb to the top of the pyramid there. I still want to have a beautiful crystal chandelier hanging over my dining room table. And, I haven't given up on seeing a Broadway show in New York City. Those things haven't happened yet, but it's fun to dream and think about the day when I can cross them off, too. I've been adding to my list by capturing the wishes and thoughts in my mind and writing them on that piece of paper.

It's your turn to grab a pen and begin to make your bucket list. Be playful about it and have fun! What would you love to do? There must be someplace in this world that you would love to visit in your lifetime: the Eiffel Tower, the Sydney Opera House, or the Great Wall of China? Is there something that you would like to do, learn, or accomplish before you kick the bucket? Skydiving, meeting your soul mate, or writing a book? In a notebook, you might write it in the form of a list or collect pictures representing the places you want to visit and the things you want to do. There are no rules about how many things should be on the list. Just get it started and add more ideas as time goes on. I encourage you to create your list and then reflect on it every once in a while. At least once a year, take a look and check the things off that you've already completed. You'll see that it's not so hard to begin dreaming again! By writing your bucket list, you are setting foot onto the raceway and taking that first step on your road to sweet success.

Your Top 101+

Next, you're going to pull in a little bit closer to dream about what you want to do or achieve within the next few years. In his book, *The Success Principles*, Jack Canfield invites readers to create a list of the top 101+ things that they want to be, do, or have. To get a clearer focus about your hopes and dreams, take a piece of paper, fold it into three equal sections, and at the top of the columns write the following: Things I Want To Be, Things I Want To Do, and Things I Want To Have. For each column, start making a list of ideas. At first the ideas are going to be flowing freely, but after a while it may start to get more difficult to come up with new ideas. You'll slow down, and you're really going to have to think hard. It's when you're concentrating that the real gold will start to reveal itself; you'll discover things that maybe you didn't know you wanted to be, do, or have. This is a wonderful exercise to dig deep into what you desire and to decide what you really want out of your life.

Here are some ideas to stimulate your creativity:

- **What do you want to be?** Maybe you want to be an author. Do you want to be a top sales producer? Maybe you want to be a speaker and travel the world. Or maybe you want to be an award-winning consultant. Focus on the roles that would help you feel fulfilled. Are there contributions to your industry or community that would fill a sense of purpose for you?

- **What do you want to do?** Do you want to create an online information product? Would you like to write a musical? You might have an adventurous spirit that wants to skydive, zip line, or bungee jump. Do you want to travel to another country? Think about the personal accomplishments you would love to achieve in the next 5-10 years.

- **What do you want to have?** Do you have a dream car in mind? Maybe it's a Mercedes or a Bentley. Do you have your sights set on that dream home? Can you imagine a piece of art by your favorite artist hanging above your fireplace? It could even be a new friend who would enrich your life. Begin to imagine the possessions that would make your life easier, more comfortable, or more enjoyable.

Focused Dreaming Activity

As racers enter the track, they know exactly where they are headed. They have a clear destination in sight. Do you know exactly where you are going? This next dreaming activity will help you uncover your next finish line. You will focus on what you want to achieve or accomplish **this year**. As you discover the goals that are within your reach, get ready to fasten your seat belt and start your engine.

> **"Without leaps of imagination or dreaming,**
> **we lose the excitement of possibilities. Dreaming,**
> **after all is a form of planning."**
>
> ~ Gloria Steinem

I complete this next brainstorming activity on a quarterly basis or when I feel like I want to create something new. I originally learned about this process in Sonia Choquette's book, *Creating Your Heart's Desire*, and it's been key for me to identify my goals ever since! Grab a piece of paper or a journal and find a comfortable, quiet place to begin focusing. For each of the eight categories below, list 3-5 ideas. Let your thoughts flow and write down whatever comes to mind.

Your Physical Body and Health: What is it about your body—your physical health—that you'd like to change this year? How can you improve your physical self? Do you want to be able to fit into a certain dress or pair of pants? Do you want to do something athletic, maybe run in a marathon? What is it about you physically that you'd like to change? It could even be your hairstyle.

Your Financial Health: Think about what you want your financial situation to look like in the near future. Do you want to have a certain amount of money in your savings account? Do you want to save up that down payment for your dream car or dream house? Do you want a raise at work? Is there a certain revenue goal that you want to hit this year? Are you looking for more regular, consistent income coming in for you each month?

Your Home: Is there something about your home that you can change to improve your immediate physical environment? Would it make you happy to clean out the garage? Do you want to renovate your kitchen? Are you ready to move to a new home? Is it time for new landscaping in the backyard?

Your Relationships: How can you improve your relationships with others? Is there a relationship that needs to be mended? Is there a new relationship that you want to create? Are you looking for a friendship, a new partner, or maybe the love of your life? It could even be that you are searching for a pet, a new "furry friend" to be your companion.

Your Job/Career: What is it in your career that you want to accomplish this year? Maybe it's doing some rebranding for your company or creating a new website. Maybe it's hitting a new revenue goal. Is it time to search for a new job that brings you more fulfillment? Do you desire a promotion? Maybe you wish to master a new skill by enrolling in continuing education classes.

Your Creative Expression: Is there something that you desire to produce to express your creativity? Maybe it's doing something artistic: take a painting class, learn to play an instrument, create a scrapbook from a recent vacation. Your creative expression could also be in the form of writing a poem, a blog, a book, or simply a personal journal. What do you wish to create?

Your Travel: Do you have any ideas for travel? Is there somewhere you want to go? Maybe a short trip or an extended vacation? Imagine traveling to that country you've been secretly wishing to visit. Are you seeking adventure or relaxation during your travel? Do you desire traveling in a new way, such as taking a train, private jet, or cruise ship? The sky's the limit! Well, maybe... do you want to ride in a rocket ship?

Your Entertainment: You work so hard and have so many responsibilities. Let all of that go for a few minutes and let your mind think about the kind of fun and excitement you'd like to experience. Maybe your spirit feels the urge to dance more! Is there a family adventure that you want to go on together? A laser tag battle? Trying karaoke for the first time? What if you could rent out a theater so you and your friends can view the latest blockbuster hit together? What do you want to do for fun this year? Go ahead and let loose, it's okay! Your work and the dirty dishes will still be there tomorrow.

After you've gone through this exercise, look over all of your ideas and start circling the ones that pop out at you. As you read through your list, some ideas will make you think, "This is what I want to focus on," or "This is what I want to do next." Generally, I end up circling 8-10 ideas. Now, you're getting even clearer about what you want to achieve.

CHOOSING YOUR GOALS

Sonia Choquette teaches, "The definition of success is to do the next thing." Success is a series of achieving things in a step-by-step manner. What is it that you want to do **next**?

> **"Setting goals is the first step in turning the invisible into the visible."**
>
> ~ Tony Robbins

Now, go through the columns and put a star next to the 1-3 items you want to focus on while reading this book and working through these principles. You're going to put a lot of effort into these goals, and you'll need to give them your full attention, time, and energy. If you choose more than three, you are at risk of spreading your energy too thin. Now is the time to get really focused, and the other ideas will still be there for your next round of dreaming and the process of selecting your top goals!

You might be thinking, "I have so many things that I want to accomplish. How do I narrow down my long list to only three?" Just because you're focusing on three doesn't mean the others aren't going to happen. You're not abandoning them. It might not be the time just yet. Here are some tips for how you can narrow down that long list of your desires:

- **Look for an umbrella goal.** Can you group any of your ideas together under one umbrella goal? Thinking of a broader, more general goal allows you to group a few of your smaller goals into one bigger goal.

- **Select the time-sensitive goal.** Are there any ideas that are time sensitive, that you must prioritize and accomplish first? The goal you choose might have a sense of urgency such as needing something buttoned up before a vacation or getting ready for that class reunion coming up around the corner!

- **Take the next step.** Are there a series of goals that must be accomplished in a certain order or in a sequential manner? Look at them in a linear fashion and start with the first one. Success is simply a series of smaller accomplishments that equal to the bigger success over time.

- **Pick the lowest-hanging fruit.** Which of your goals is the juiciest, ripest peach on the tree? You'll know, because you'll look at the goal and think, "Yes, this is the one that is standing out!" It's raising its hand saying, "Pick me! Pick me!"

Once you've successfully narrowed down your list, the next step is to look at the one, two, or three goals you've selected and ask yourself these three questions:

1. **Can I achieve this goal within six months to a year?** You'll want to focus on goals you believe you can achieve within a year, even better yet, within six months.

2. **Is this MY true heart's desire?** Your goal must be something that you really want to do and create, regardless of what anybody else around you thinks or is pushing you to do. You must have a deep desire to go after this goal.

3. **Will I and can I show up to this goal each and every day?** A strong desire to show up to your goal each and every day is critical to your success. You'll want to give the goal your full attention.

If you answered "no" to any of the questions regarding your goals, think about selecting a new one. Don't waste your time on a goal that doesn't have a chance from the get-go.

Now that your goals have been selected and you have your sights set on the finish line, you will want to ensure the smoothest ride possible. Writing your goals on paper will set an intention for you and get you off to a great start. As you write them, consider some tips to make sure they are written in the most effective way possible:

Write your goals in a positive manner.

Be intentional about using positive words when writing your goals. During a goal-setting session with a client, I review their written goals, paying close attention to word choice. Instead of looking at the negative, such as "We maintain a monthly customer **complaint** rate of less than 20%," ask yourself how you can make it more positive. You're going to find that you get more of what you focus on, so instead of focusing on the negative, simply flip it to the positive so it reads, "We maintain a monthly **satisfaction** rate of 80%." Instead of thinking about how much weight you want to lose, write a goal that specifies how much you'd like to weigh. If that messy garage is at the top of your list, write a goal that focuses on how clean and tidy you want that garage to be. Think about exactly what you DO want, not what you DON'T want.

Examples:

- We maintain a monthly <u>customer satisfaction</u> rate of 80%.
- I am at my <u>ideal</u> weight of 135 pounds.
- My garage is <u>neat, clean, and organized.</u>

Be sure your goals have pure intentions.

The goals you choose to pursue should support your soul's purpose and be genuinely sincere, kind, and true to who you are. Your main motivation of achieving them should be to become a better version of you. During The Big Drive, it wasn't that I wanted to beat the other partners who were the top salesmen that year. It was about me achieving something that I had never done before. The accomplishment of your goal should lead to a more fulfilling life for you and those who will also be impacted in a positive way. Your goals should never be rooted in greed or jealousy and should not take away from another. Instead of wanting to make more money than someone else, have a better car than your neighbor, or achieve something just to make a person jealous, write your goals from a place of pure intent.

Examples:

- This year my company is thriving and impacting the lives of many while generating $1 million in revenue.
- I am driving and enjoying the car of <u>my dreams</u>!
- I am proud to be a member of the best-selling author community.

Write your goals in the present tense.

Instead of using phrases such as "I will" or "I'm going to," try writing your goals in the present tense. Use "I am" phrases to get you thinking in the here and now. You'll find that you get what you focus on, so if you are talking in the future, those goals might always remain in your future. It may seem hard to think this way, because it's not true at the moment or in alignment with your current circumstances. But I always say, "Fake it 'til you make it." Keep reading and repeating your goals in the present tense to help them become your reality faster.

Examples:

- <u>I am</u> the award-winning "Marketer of the Year."
- <u>I am vacationing</u> with my family in Australia this year.
- <u>I am the owner</u> of a four-bedroom home in my dream neighborhood.

Your goals should allow for the plus factor.

Sometimes we put limits on ourselves, when in fact there could be something even better around the corner. When writing your goals, add in room for the universe to bring you something bigger and better than you can even imagine at this moment. Add a "plus" to a metric or number goal or add in the phrases "more" or "better" to build in the plus factor. You never know, you just may be surprised at the opportunities that come your way! Don't create any boundaries, ceilings, or limits on what you can achieve. Maybe there's a better job, a nicer home, or more sales coming your way!

Examples:

- I earn <u>$250,000+</u> of take-home pay each year.
- I have 20 <u>or more</u> speaking gigs booked this year.
- I am the general manager of JKL Company <u>or better</u>.

Now that you've written the perfect goals, it's time to display them! Print them out or write them on a sheet of paper and tape them to your bathroom mirror, near your desk, or by your bed stand. They should be located in a place where you can see them, read them, and internalize them multiple times each day. Declare them over and over again to begin manifesting them in your life.

TAKING THE LEAP

"Everything you want is just outside your comfort zone."

~ Robert Allen

Are you ready to take the leap? You've been dreaming and have uncovered your heart's desires. You've written your goals and can feel the excitement bubbling up inside of you. This is as far as some people get on the road to their goal achievement. You might be wondering, "What if I fail?" My question back to you is, "What do you have to lose?" I understand that taking the leap can be hard for some. Maybe you're used to playing it safe and wondering why you should bother taking the risk. It's time to step outside of your comfort zone. Some will hesitate and think, "This scares me. I've made this huge commitment, and I don't know how I'll be able to make it happen." Don't let that be you! This book is filled with tips and strategies to help you make your dreams come true. You'll learn how to manage your fear and equip yourself with doubt busters to keep you moving forward. The saying goes, "If you're not growing, you're dying." Take the chance to learn, grow, and live out your deepest desires.

You also might be thinking, "How in the world am I going to do this? It seems so impossible!" At this point, I don't want you to concern yourself with the details about **how** it's going to happen. You have selected your goals because you have a deep desire to achieve them. The "how" will come once you have the right mindset, make the right preparations, and start moving toward the goals. At the start of The Big Drive contest, I had absolutely no idea how I was going to sell all that I needed to sell in order to win. In my entire career, I had only sold a handful of Infusionsoft subscriptions. I had no plan for how this time would be any different. However, the "what" and the "why" were crystal clear. I knew that I wanted to be number one and win that car to show myself I could do anything I set my mind to. Many people give up and fail before they even set out on their journey because they get intimidated and hung up on the "how." Right now simply focus on what you want and why you want it.

Dare to go after your dreams. Go ahead and take the leap. Push yourself to get out of your comfort zone, even slightly. I believe you've got what it takes to achieve your goals and this book will help get you there! Your time has come. Your time is now, so get in the driver's seat, buckle up, and start your engine! The race is just about to begin, and it's your turn to join in. The warm-up laps are underway and soon they'll be dropping the green flag to signify the start of your race. It's going to be a thrilling and memorable ride!

GET INTO GEAR

- Start to dream again by creating your bucket list and writing your list of the 101+ things you want to be, do, or have.

- The "Focused Dreaming Activity" will help you think about what you'd like to achieve in your career, personal life, physical health and financial health in the next year.

- Circle goals that stand out and ask yourself the three vital questions as you narrow your list down to no more than three goals.

- Select and write your goals by positioning them in a positive manner, creating them with pure intentions, using present tense phrases, and allowing for the plus factor.

- Get out of your comfort zone by taking the leap to pursue your dreams and desires.

- Don't worry about the "how." Focus on the "what" and the "why" as you set out on your journey.

ACCELERATE TOWARD YOUR SUCCESS

1. Purchase a journal or a special notebook for your reflections and ideas as you commit to your goals. I encourage you to make a special trip and head to Target, the Hallmark store, the Dollar Tree, or an office supply store. Make it a point to find something new and fun to write in as you work through this book. Browse through the selection of notebooks and journals and look for a cover that speaks to you. It could be your favorite color, have the perfect quote or saying, or have an image or design that makes you think of your road to sweet success. This will be the very first step you take toward the finish line!

2. Complete the "Focused Dreaming Activity" and narrow your ideas down to your top three goals. Practice writing them in the most effective way possible by following the guidelines in this chapter. Clarity is essential to starting your journey on the right foot.

ON THE ROAD REFLECTIONS

Make a commitment to your dreams today by making a declaration. Write your goals in the pages of your new journal and begin to script how your life will be different or change positively by achieving each of them. This will help you focus on WHAT you want and WHY you want it. Write as if your goals have already been achieved. What is your life like? How is it different? Let your mind explore the possibilities as you write and reflect.

**Right now, simply focus on WHAT you want
and WHY you want it.**

CHAPTER

PREPARE TO QUALIFY

"Just as your car runs more smoothly and requires less energy to go faster and farther when the wheels are in perfect alignment, you perform better when your thoughts, feelings, emotions, goals, and values are in balance."

~ Brian Tracy

Before you check in for the race to your goals, you must make sure you are in peak performance for the long road ahead. Just as a race car driver needs to pass inspection, you too need to show you are ready to race. The most important gauge to monitor is how you feel about achieving your goals. Your belief must be at the right level if you want to have a chance at crossing the finish line. Get ready to monitor your dashboard and gauges to check the level of your belief and the power of your emotions. Learn how to utilize a six-point tune-up to make sure you are in tip-top shape. You can't win if you can't race. You can't race if you don't qualify. And you can't qualify if you don't pass inspection. The key is to believe in yourself, to believe that you've got what it takes to win! Once you pass your inspection with the right levels of belief, you'll receive your final sticker and will qualify for the race.

I THINK I CAN, I THINK I CAN, I THINK I CAN...

So many times I would set off toward a goal, only to come to a screeching stop as I pulled away from the starting line. Thoughts like, "This is going to be hard!" or "I'm not sure I've got what it takes," would enter my mind. The self-doubt would creep in, steal my dreams, and I'd give up before I even began. The Big Drive was not the first sales contest hosted by Infusionsoft. The company had many other contests before. Once in a while, I'd give it the old "girl scout" try to win a cash bonus or some other prize. But, right out of the gates, I would see the regular top salespeople start racking up sales on the leaderboard, leaving me in the dust. My one or two sales looked like amateur night. I remember throwing in the towel while telling myself, the dog, my husband, and my computer screen, "I don't even have a chance! It's not fair. I'll never win. I GIVE UP!" This lack of confidence and defeatist attitude did not serve me well at all. Of course I had a chance. I simply didn't believe in my ability to sell in large numbers at one time.

This time I had committed myself to accomplishing this really big, hairy, audacious goal of winning the car and coming home with the grand prize. I knew I needed to get myself to actually believe that I could, in fact, win. This time had to be different. I needed to believe in myself and have faith that it was possible for me to sell more than anyone else. I made the conscious effort to get to a state of belief and tried a few different ways to trick my brain into believing I could do this.

I began by remembering my past successes and thought of some of the big things I already accomplished in my life. I looked through old scrapbooks and photo albums and started feeling really good about myself. I came across a high school report card with straight A's. I remembered back to the day when I committed to having all A's that quarter. I put in extra effort in all of my classes, kept track of every graded assignment, and completed extra credit to pull it off. That was a great accomplishment for me, and it brought back the feeling of pride for a job well done. I also found a picture from the time I was named "Teacher of the Year" in the city where I worked as an elementary school teacher. I thought back to the day the principal gathered all of the teachers in the hallway before school started and announced I had received this award. My hard work and dedication to my teaching career had been recognized. I felt honored and proud. Reminiscing and recalling some of the other "nearly impossible" things I achieved in my life made me feel empowered and confident to stay in the game and go for the Camaro.

After declaring that I would win the car, I started to do some research to find out about the details of the contest. I needed to know exactly what would be required of me to win. I read the contest details online to discover the dates, qualifying sales, and other rules. Then I called my dedicated sales rep, Cory Bendixen, at Infusionsoft to do a little more digging and gain some insight about what it would take to win. I asked him, "Who were the key players during last year's contest? How many software subscriptions did they sell? In what time frame did they do it? How many subscriptions will I need to sell to win this whole thing?" Cory did a little research, got back to me, and said that for those three months, they felt that the person who would sell 50 subscriptions would take the prize. Now I had a specific goal, something to work with, and I started mapping out a plan. I took the number 50, and I broke it down. I created a chart showing how many subscriptions I needed to sell each month and then each week. After breaking that big number down into smaller pieces, it wasn't as daunting. This exercise helped me see that, "Yeah, this is possible. I can do this." My belief in myself got a little stronger.

Then, I found a leaderboard online that Infusionsoft had posted with the names and total number of sales for the top producers. Just as I kept track of my grades in high school the quarter I wanted straight A's, this leaderboard was going to help me keep an eye on what the others were doing and how I ranked on a daily basis. I even took a screenshot of the leaderboard and superimposed my name in the number one spot with the number 50 next it. I glued this image to a poster board and tacked it up next to my desk so I could see my name there in the number one place, even if maybe the real statistics weren't showing that at the time. Although the contest hadn't officially started, by doing my due diligence, I felt productive and ahead of the game. I was gaining confidence in myself! I could hardly contain my excitement!

Because of my love of music, I thought it would be fun to pick songs that were going to motivate and empower me every day. I wanted inspiring music that would cheer me up and keep pushing me throughout the contest. The first song that resonated with me was "Roar" by Katy Perry:

I got the eye of the tiger, a fighter

Dancing through the fire

'Cause I am a champion, and you're gonna hear me roar

Louder, louder than a lion

'Cause I am a champion, and you're gonna hear me roar!

Listening and singing along to this song made me feel really powerful, assertive, and courageous. I loved its message, "Here I am, everybody! I'm here and you're going to hear me roar!" Every time I heard it, this song evoked emotions of strength and personal power from within as I declared, "It is my time to stand firm, give it my all, and show the world I am a champion." I wasn't going to "bite my tongue and hold my breath" or sit quietly in the background this time. Instead, like Katy Perry sang, I was going to come in with a roar so loud everyone would hear me and respect me as I dominated this contest.

I also did a YouTube search to find songs that featured a Camaro, and I discovered that there was a song by Rascal Flatts called "Red Camaro." It was such an upbeat song, and it was so perfect to be my theme song during The Big Drive. The song talks about "cruising in your Camaro with the top down in the summer," which helped me think of myself enjoying the ride in my own Camaro:

Turn up the music loud

Take the T-tops out

And let the chrome shine

Cruise along the riverside

As I listened to this song, I imagined myself driving along a beautiful winding road in the warmth of a summer day with the wind blowing through my hair. It filled me with positive energy, joy, and pride of all I was going to accomplish during this journey. This was a song that would keep me focusing on the end result and imagining that I had already won the car.

I made it a habit to tell myself I could do it and often thought to myself or said aloud, "I believe that car is mine. I am the grand prize winner of The Big Drive." This was my intention, and I worked to maintain this state of belief by checking in with my emotions every day. I couldn't, not even for one second, let go of my belief. Achieving this confidence in myself was crucial for me to start off on the right foot. I eagerly awaited the official start of the contest so I could hit the road and set out on the journey toward my sweet success.

MONITOR YOUR DASHBOARD

"Believe you can and you're halfway there."

~ Theodore Roosevelt

Just as a car needs to be in optimal condition for peak performance in the race, so do you! The first gauge you need to check on your dashboard is the level of your belief. Do you truly believe that you can achieve this goal? This is actually the hardest part as you set off on your journey. Once you get to a state of belief, then you're halfway there. I want you to really think about believing in that goal and believing that you have what it takes to achieve it. You wouldn't have that desire if there wasn't a seed inside that convinced you to go for it. The seed of belief already exists, so I'm going to help you identify that belief and make it an even stronger feeling for you.

You may be wondering, "How do I achieve a state of belief?" First you need to start by identifying how you feel about the possibility of achieving your goal and go from there. Does it cause you anxiety to think about the hard work in front of you? Do you feel discouraged by your current situation? Are you hopeful that it's within your reach? Each feeling has a place on Esther Hick's "Emotional Guidance Scale." This scale is a tool for you to use daily to gauge how you feel and what you need to do to get to positive expectation and belief. Let's take a look:

The Emotional Guidance Scale

1. Joy/Appreciation/Empowered/Freedom/Love

2. Passion

3. Enthusiasm/Eagerness/Happiness

4. Positive Expectation/Belief

5. Optimism

6. Hopefulness

7. Contentment

8. Boredom

9. Pessimism

10. Frustration/Irritation/Impatience

11. "Overwhelment"

12. Disappointment

13. Doubt

14. Worry

15. Blame

16. Discouragement

17. Anger

18. Revenge

19. Hatred/Rage

20. Jealousy

21. Insecurity/Guilt/Unworthiness

22. Fear/Grief/Depression/Despair/Powerlessness

Source: Esther and Jerry Hicks, *Ask and It Is Given: Learning to Manifest Your Desires* (United States: Hay House, Inc. 2004). Page 114.

You can use this scale to gauge your emotions and identify how you're feeling at any given time, especially how you're feeling about achieving your goal. If you fall below a #7 (contentment) and slip into boredom, frustration, doubt, or any of the other emotions that follow, the "check gauges" light should come on to warn you to get to a better feeling place. Awareness of your emotional level is key and crucial to your success. When you are aware of a fault, weakness, or obstacle, then you have the ability to fix it and navigate around it!

You're going to attract more of the same into your life that is something similar to the feeling that you have. When you feel fear, more fear will come upon you. If you feel gratitude, more things that you can be grateful for will appear in your life. For example, have you ever had one of those really horrible days where you've been frustrated and things don't seem to be going your way? You can't find your keys in the morning and you've got to get to an appointment. Your feelings of frustration and impatience are growing. Then, all of a sudden you find yourself engulfed in standstill traffic, and you grow even more impatient! On the other hand, if you're having a really great day or successful week, it seems like the good luck keeps coming your way and things seem to be getting better every minute of every day.

We all have bad days and will experience negative emotions from time to time. That's okay. There's no need to be afraid of your feelings. It's important to keep moving up the Emotional Guidance Scale until you experience a positive emotion. You need to be very conscious about where you are on the Emotional Guidance Scale and keep trying to get to a better feeling place. During my private coaching calls or group sessions, I ask questions to find out how my clients are feeling about achieving their goals. Once I guide them to identify the best word to describe the feeling, then I work on moving them up the scale by giving them tools and strategies. One of the best ways to level up is to simply do something that you love: play with your dog, call your best friend, or dig in to a bucket of ice cream!

A SIX-STEP TUNE-UP

> "To accomplish great things, we must not only act,
> but also dream, not only plan, but also believe."
>
> ~ Anatole France

Before any car can go on a track for the race, it must receive a final sticker signifying that it has passed inspection. You need to perform a tune-up to ensure operation at peak efficiency for your race to the finish. Build your faith, trust, and confidence in yourself by making a few general adjustments:

Step 1: Know Who You Are
As you prepare to set out on the road to your desires, realize that

the achievement of your goals will allow you to become more of who you already are. You will become a better version of "you" throughout this journey, so take some time to reflect on who you are. What are the qualities that set you apart from everyone else? What do you bring to the table? Focusing on your positive personality traits will help you build your self-confidence and get to that state of belief that you'll crush your goals.

One early assignment I give my coaching clients is to contact people you respect and admire, and ask them to describe you in one word. Reach out with an email, text, or private message and continue asking around until you get 10 different words. As the adjectives begin to come in, create a document for recording them. Look up the definitions and write the meaning next to each word.

Here are the 10 words I received when completing this activity:

- **Charismatic** - Possessing an extraordinary ability to attract, capable of influencing or inspiring large numbers of people, inspires great enthusiasm and devotion

- **Methodical** - Orderly and systematic in thought or behavior

- **Energetic** - Powerful in action or effect, forceful, effective

- **Determined** - Of unwavering mind, resolute, strongly motivated to succeed, ambitious

- **Dedicated** - Devoted, wholly committed to a cause, ideal, or personal goal

- **Successful** - Having obtained something desired or intended, having succeeded in one's endeavors

- **Effervescent** - High-spirited, vivacious, full of life and energy

- **Courageous** - Willing to undertake or seek out new and daring enterprises, fearless, daring

- **Focused** - Close or narrow attention, concentration

- **Inspirational** - To stimulate to action, to motivate, to produce or arouse a feeling or thought, to influence or impel

It's a major confidence booster to discover and reflect on other people's impressions of you. I never would have described myself as charismatic or effervescent, but after reading the definitions,

I thought, "Yes! Those words describe me perfectly!" Have fun with this activity, express gratitude for the feedback, and let the responses empower you to believe in yourself. These can become wonderful "I Am" statements that you can repeat to yourself in times of doubt. "I am dedicated. I am courageous. I am successful." Knowing and claiming who you are is a powerful first step in getting to a state of belief.

Step 2: Remember Your Past Successes

When you remember all of the wonderful things that you've achieved in your life, you're going to see that you already are a successful person. You have been achieving your desires your entire life. Think back to times when you overcame obstacles that you thought were impossible at one point. What are you really proud of accomplishing? This is a really great way for you to get to belief as well. Remember how awesome you already are and the incredible things that you've already done.

Have you:

- Earned a degree or certification that was difficult to obtain?

- Started your own business?

- Experienced special events in your life such as getting married, becoming a parent, or buying a home?

- Mastered a skill or developed a talent?

- Taken some really awesome vacations?

- Received awards or special acknowledgements for a job well done?

- Hit certain milestones in your work or business?

- Put yourself out there and taken a risk that resulted in success?

Keep brainstorming and create a list of your top successes in your journal. Then, surround yourself with reminders of the items that you're most proud of achieving in your life. You can display pictures from those events above your fireplace, near your desk, or as your screensaver. Maybe there are different tokens, trophies, or mementos you can also look at to remember those achievements.

Put these items on your desk, on a shelf, on your walls, or on your dresser. Look at them often to bring up the memory and feeling of accomplishing your goals. Think of all that you overcame to achieve them and how proud you are for that. You are already an excellent creator and should realize that this situation is no different!

Step 3: Do Your Due Diligence

Find out as much as you can about the goals you want to achieve by doing some background research. Ask questions and look for answers, scrub the Internet for articles that can help you, and carefully examine the process from all angles.

Let's imagine that one of your goals is to write a book. Do some investigating and find resources to help you determine the best practices for writing, publishing, and launching your book. Conduct research online and purchase books to help you learn more about this topic. Interview others who have accomplished the same goal and ask them about their experience. What worked well? What would they change if they did it again? You'll find that people are willing to help and share, so reach out to gain some wisdom and encouragement from them. Let's say your goal is to enter a contest or competition. Dig in and review the rules and qualifications. Take the time to study previous winners. What did they produce to become the winner? Watch their videos, examine their work, and listen to their story. This will arm you with tactics and strategies to get it done, and it will build your confidence at the same time.

While doing your research and due diligence, you will discover what it's going to take to achieve the goal. When you gain a general idea of the path you'll need to follow and hear success stories from others who have accomplished something similar, you're going to find that maybe it's not as daunting as you first thought. You're going to strengthen your belief because you now see it as possible. You now realize that your goal is within your reach.

Step 4: Outline a Simple Plan

Now, it's time to chunk it down! You have this big, lofty goal and so much work ahead of you that it may seem overwhelming. Breaking it down into smaller steps and creating a **simple** plan is going to show you that it's actually possible to achieve your goal and give you a track to run on. Think high-level planning, keep it very general at this point and don't get stuck on too many details quite yet.

When I began writing this book, I had a general plan to follow:

- Brainstorm ideas, examples, and stories to include in the book.

- Narrow down the ideas and finalize the chapter structure.

- Develop and write the content for each chapter.

- Revise and edit the draft.

- Design the book cover and page layout format.

- Develop an email and social media marketing plan.

- Create a landing page for the book launch.

- Schedule podcasts, interviews, and book signings.

- Plan a celebration dinner with my family.

Once I had my simple plan, I created a timeline by setting due dates for each item on the list. I began blocking off dates for the big milestones in my calendar and creating time in my weekly schedule to focus on this project. This process helped me think practically and got me really excited about the process of reaching my goal! You can do the same for any project or endeavor you pursue. Think of the steps you'll need to complete as you prepare for your dream vacation, move into your new home, or launch that new website. Your goal achievement will seem doable and manageable, and your new plan will serve as a roadmap to guide your journey.

Step 5: Use Music to Lift Your Spirits

Music, the language of emotion, has a powerful way of evoking specific feelings. It can make you laugh, feel adventurous, fall in love, and even cry with joy. Uplifting songs are a great way to feel better. It can also make you feel sad or lonely, so be careful about listening to sad country songs about getting dumped, being mistreated or misled because that's not going to move you up the Emotional Guidance Scale. In fact, it could have the opposite effect and actually worsen your mood. Make it a habit to listen to music that inspires you, lifts you up, and gets you feeling positive and energized.

Music can change your emotions in a split second. You can listen to it while you're cooking, while you're driving, or while you're in the shower. Don't be shy! You can even dance and have fun with it, too. Before attending a meeting, hosting a webinar, having a call with a new prospect, or facilitating a group coaching call, I take a few minutes and listen to a song that gets me feeling pumped up and excited. You can do this too! Whatever your favorite music is, it could be 80s hair bands, Elvis, or anything that makes you happy, have that playlist in your car, on your computer, or on your iPod. Use a streaming app like Pandora, Songza, or Spotify to help you have that genre of music in the background when you need a pick-me-up. Even better, go a step further and select a theme song that's very specific to your goal.

Here are some of my clients' favorite theme songs:

- "Don't Stop Believing" - Journey
- "Incredible" - Ne-Yo and Celine Dion
- "Happy" - Pharrell
- "Firework" - Katy Perry
- "Feel This Moment" - Pit Bull featuring Christina Aguilera
- "Dreams" - Van Halen
- "The Climb" - Miley Cyrus
- "Geronimo" - Sheppard
- "Eye of the Tiger" - Survivor
- "Born Free" - Kid Rock
- "Remember the Name" - Fort Minor
- "On Top of the World" - Imagine Dragons
- "Brighter than the Sun" - Colbie Caillat
- "Best Day of My Life" - American Authors

I worked with a private coaching client, who had entered a marketer of the year contest. The first thing I did was give her three tasks to boost her confidence. One of them was to pick her theme song. Lisa knew right from the beginning that "Happy" by Pharrell was her song. She went out for a run and was feeling really happy but very scared about being chosen as one of the contest finalists. She put the song on her iPod and began listening to it while she ran. As she began to feel a very strong feeling of absolute gratitude, she stopped in her tracks and began to cry. That's how physical it was. After that, she was so deeply connected to the song and she yearned to feel the sense of complete gratitude every day. Lisa gave herself a few minutes each morning to listen to her theme song. As she closed her eyes, she started seeing the incredible blessings in her life and feeling gratitude about everything. This daily practice helped her achieve a state of belief that she could win.

I want you to create a deep connection with your song, too. It may not evoke feelings of gratitude like it did for Lisa. Instead it may empower you to feel strength, power, happiness, or another feeling high on the Emotional Guidance Scale. Just listen and FEEL.

My theme songs change with the different goals that I have. However, whenever I hear any of my theme songs, they help me remember those past successes. I'll hear "Roar" by Katy Perry on the radio, and it brings me back to The Big Drive. It reminds me of that powerful feeling. Pick your song and let it keep you motivated to stay in the race!

Step 6: Repeat "I Believe" Statements

One of the most effective tools that I've found working with my clients for achieving a state of belief is writing and repeating "I Believe" statements. Repeat these affirmations in your daily conversations with your family members, friends, colleagues, and partners.

What do you believe you can do? Here are some prompts for you to begin your list:

I believe I've got what it takes to win.

I believe I can write a book.

I believe my time is now and this is my year to shine.

I believe I'm surpassing my revenue goals.

I believe that vacation is within my reach.

I believe I'm a talented songwriter with a hit song.

I believe I'm a smart business person who is leading my company to be a $10 million+ company this year.

When listing your "I Believe" statements, remember the checklist you used when writing your goals. Write them in a positive manner, have pure intentions, keep them in the present tense, and allow for that plus factor. As you begin to say your "I Believe" statements in your daily interactions with others, there might be a disconnect in what you're saying and how you actually feel. Don't worry, "fake it 'til you make it!" Just keep repeating them, and in a short time you're going to get to that state of belief.

> **"Whether you think you can or you think you can't, you're right."**
>
> ~ Henry Ford

While hosting a creative workshop for an executive team, I facilitated a session that guided the team to individually write their "I Believe" statements about hitting their quarterly metrics. A couple of weeks later I visited the team again. One of the leaders had invited his whole department to write their "I Believe" statements on brightly colored sticky notes and add them to a large poster board hanging in their workspace. I was so thrilled to see him get his staff involved in this activity. It boosted morale and got everyone on board with smashing their goals.

Once you start repeating these statements over and over, things are going to change quickly for you. I've seen it in my personal experiences. I've seen it for my family members, and I've witnessed it for the clients that I've worked with. Your "I Believe" statements are going to help you get to that state of belief and stay there. I want you to say them out loud. I want you to write them down, and I want you to post them around you. Writing and repeating "I Believe" statements is going to be a very powerful way for you to prepare for the journey ahead of you.

MAINTAINING A STATE OF BELIEF

With some practice, you can begin to believe in yourself. Once you've achieved a state a belief, you need to maintain it. No matter what comes your way, you have to continue to believe. Disbelief is one of your worst enemies on the road to your success. When you drop a few levels on the Emotional Guidance Scale and start to feel boredom, frustration, or disappointment, it's important to acknowledge that feeling and take back control of your emotions. The best way to feel better quickly is to simply do something you love!

- Listen to your theme song.
- Read your "I Believe" statements.
- Engage in a favorite hobby.
- Spend time with friends.
- Watch a funny movie or television show.
- Move your body with some light exercise.
- Take a walk.
- Play with your pet.
- Sing and dance to a favorite song.

It's somewhat likely that while you are gaining confidence in yourself, telling others about your plans, and sharing your "I Believe" statements, some people (maybe even those really close to you) are going to raise their eyebrows and tell you not to get your hopes up. Beware the naysayer! Don't let someone else's comments squash your dreams. When I started declaring I was going to win the car, I was bombarded with doubtful reactions. I didn't let those faze me. I simply ignored each skeptical or negative comment, and I kept looking for my supporters. No one was going to get in the way of me achieving my goal. Some people simply don't wish success for others but don't let them stop you dead in your tracks. In the coming chapters, you will learn how to overcome specific obstacles. Until then, don't stop believing in yourself!

GET INTO GEAR

- Understand that belief is a key component of your goal achievement.

- Use the Emotional Guidance Scale to identify how you're feeling about achieving your goals.

- Remember your past successes and surround yourself with reminders of them.

- Do research and create a simple plan that will help you work toward accomplishing your goals.

- Become aware of negative feelings and focus on activities that help you feel better.

ACCELERATE TOWARD YOUR SUCCESS

1. Remember your past successes. Write a list of the top 4-5 accomplishments you are most proud of and create something to display these achievements. It could be a picture collage, a small scrapbook, or even an arrangement of tokens and photos on a shelf. While you look at your display each day, reflect back on those special moments and feel the sense of pride. This will empower you to feel more confident in your ability to achieve your new goals.

2. Select your theme song. Choose a song that reminds you of your goal achievement. As you listen to it daily, it will give you the strength, motivation, and encouragement you'll need as you move toward your goals.

ON THE ROAD REFLECTIONS

Take some time to write a list of "I Believe" statements in your journal such as: I believe I've got what it takes to achieve my goals, I believe success is within my reach, and I believe success is flowing to me freely. Get very specific about your goal achievement. Make it a habit to read them aloud to yourself daily. Soon you'll internalize these statements, develop more confidence in yourself, and create new beliefs about what you feel you can accomplish.

**Believe that you have what it takes
to achieve your goals.**

CHAPTER

ASSEMBLE YOUR PIT CREW

"Talent wins games, but teamwork and intelligence wins championships."

~ Michael Jordan

E ven an outstanding driver can't cross the finish line and win the race without the help of others. A championship is never achieved without the assistance and dedication of a stellar support system. A world-class pit crew will keep you on track. They will alert you to obstacles or situations you may not be aware of. And, they will help you refuel and fix problems to keep you moving safely and swiftly on the course. Your fan base, coaches, and mentors will keep your spirits up and encourage you as you set off toward your destination. Surround yourself with a support network that will guide you to your success and cheer you on throughout this journey.

RECRUITING MY TEAM

During The Big Drive competition, I enlisted all sorts of help to keep me in motion and headed toward the grand prize. There was no way that I could have accomplished all that I did throughout those three months by myself. I surrounded myself with an incredible team. This group of people supported me, guided me, and took action right alongside me throughout my journey.

When I decided to go for this Camaro, I enlisted the help of my family. First and foremost, I told my husband, Joe, that this was something I wanted to do and that I wanted his support. As my business partner, husband, and best friend, I look to Joe to be my number one advocate. Then, we got our three children excited and on board with this competition. I wanted them to have some ownership in this goal and to play a role in this journey as well. Getting the kids involved was not only fun, but they kept me on track. There were days when the kids would come home from school and as soon as they walked in the door, they'd ask, "Mommy, did you sell any subscriptions today?" I'd have to tell them the good news or the bad news. They held me accountable. And, they supported me, even on the days that I had to make a sales call instead of swim in the pool with them. As a family unit, we were all vested in this contest. Their support and excitement fueled my desire to bring home the prize. Letting them down was not an option for me!

I started to share my goal of achieving this victory with my colleagues, friends and other family members. I brought up the contest and my desire to win the car in casual conversations with those closest to me. I knew that some would be skeptical, and that was okay. I continued searching for my fans, the people who would applaud for me from the sidelines and cheer for me all the way to the finish line. It wasn't difficult to find them, and soon I had a small base of enthusiastic fans who were genuinely rooting for me and my success. I began to regularly receive motivational messages from my cheerleaders, and I looked to them to pick me up when I was feeling down. Their positive comments, high fives, and cheers were critical in motivating me to stay on the course.

I also had my right-hand man, Cory Bendixen, my dedicated partner sales representative at Infusionsoft. I needed somebody who would be by my side, pushing me, encouraging me, and supporting me the whole way. Cory helped me right from the get-go. He met with me in person a few times to advise me on the development of the programs that I was going to offer and how to price and package my services. He was my sounding board and listened to my ideas, questions, and strategies. He worked with me on a daily basis and held me accountable to my goals. He coached me before my sales calls, researched for me, assisted me with tasks, and kept me "in-the-know" about contest happenings.

If I needed somebody to talk to, I could give Cory a call. He was always there to pick me up and push me forward. Many times he was there to give me a high five, letting me know that I did a good job. He shared in my excitement and celebrated the small wins with me along the way.

With the sudden and drastic increase in my workload, I couldn't manage it by myself. I leveraged technology by finding some of the best software programs that could help me with project management, online appointment scheduling, and virtual training systems. I recruited a team of virtual assistants and trained this amazing group of ladies to help me configure the software and replicate systems for my new clients. I trained a few marketing automation coaches who could teach the new clients to use my programs and guide them through the process of getting started. I worked closely with experts and technicians: a marketing strategist, a graphic designer, and others. I had this entire team there helping me up to the very last minute of the contest and beyond!

For guidance and motivation, I scheduled regular calls with my coaches and mentors. I wanted to have people who would hold me accountable to my goal, identify my blind spots, and give me perspective about how to learn and grow during this experience. I planned to check in with them throughout the contest for fresh insight and direction when it came to winning this contest and building my business. I felt it was inevitable that I would get stuck in a rut or hit a dead end occasionally, and I planned to confide in my coaches so they could help me overcome my obstacles. I scheduled time to meet and talk with my mentor, Trish McCarty. She always knows the right thing to say to help me get to the next level and instills a great confidence in me. I also continued meeting with my mastermind group monthly. The members of my mastermind encouraged me to think bigger, gave me bright ideas, and helped me navigate through the challenges.

With my pit crew and fan base in place, I felt completely and fully supported, like I could achieve anything and conquer my goal of winning The Big Drive.

WE DON'T CREATE ALONE

> **"Alone we can do so little,**
> **together we can do so much."**
>
> ~ Helen Keller

Nothing has ever been created alone. We are all co-creating our world together, many minds and many hands working together constantly to create. Even in the process of building a house, there are many people involved to accomplish this goal: architects, carpenters, electricians, interior designers, just to name a few. Everyone contributes in their own way and each act contributes to the creation of the final product. Realizing that we're all connected and creating together will help you notice and be receptive to the help available all around you. Just as the race car driver depends on the pit crew, you need your helpers to assist during your race to the finish.

What are the first steps to getting the assistance you need? You have to be open and receptive to asking for and to receiving help.

Be giving. The saying goes, "You get what you give," and that applies to everything in life. I always tell my clients that if you're lacking anything in your life whether it's time, money, or support, the first thing that you must do is give away that same thing. If you need more time, give your time away freely. If you want to get more help in your life, you need to first give away help to others.

Napoleon Hill said, "It is literally true that you can succeed best by helping others to succeed." That's really important, to have the mindset that success will come to you by helping others and having those pure intentions about what you're doing. To begin the process of finding help, lend a helping hand. Go out of your way to help somebody else. Be giving in your service, kind words, and encouragement with pure intentions and expect nothing in return from a particular person. Don't give to someone with the expectation that you're going to receive something back instantaneously. Remember, "What goes around comes around." Have faith that your goodness will be returned to you, maybe even multiplied. You won't even know where it's going to come from, and where it does come from might surprise you. Living with a giving spirit will attract goodness and help into your life.

Ask for help. Be open to asking for help each and every day. You don't have to be the lone wolf and go at this all by yourself. Don't be so stubborn that you feel too proud to ask for assistance. Speak up and don't be shy! Voice your needs. People are genuinely good and want to help you. I've found that help just pours in as soon as you begin looking for it.

Make it a habit to ask at least one person to help you every day. A member of one of my group coaching programs, Tracy, explained how asking for help was a game changer for her. As a homeschooling mother and work-at-home marketing specialist, she juggled quite a bit in her life as you can imagine! She began to ask for help around the house to alleviate her workload and commented, "Something amazing is happening in my house around the 'I can't do it alone' idea. My husband is now paying our daughter to clean the kitchen for me every day. The kitchen is one the hardest rooms for me to stay on top of. I can't do it alone, and this help is seriously changing my life!" Begin by identifying your needs, and start asking for the help you need.

Receive the help. Now that you've asked for help, be willing to receive it. Sometimes accepting help can be hard, because you might think, "I can do it better," or "They're not going to do it the way I want it to be done," but I encourage you to accept the help and see what happens. Once you open up to this idea, you'll be more receptive to all of the help available to you. More often you'll notice people saying, "Is there something I can do to help?" or "Can I help you?" Make it a new habit to always reply, "Yes!"

A couple of years back, I was going to present at a conference, and I didn't know what I was going to wear. After an exhausting week of shopping all over the Phoenix Valley in search of the perfect outfit, I felt frustrated and desperate. Finally, as I entered another store, a clerk welcomed me and asked if there was anything she could do to help me. I looked her right in the eye and said, "Yes! I do need help!" She asked me about the occasion and started pulling all sorts of clothing pieces and accessories for me to try on. She helped me pick out things I never would have chosen for myself, and within an hour I had the perfect ensemble. I felt like a million bucks the day of the conference up on stage wearing my blue skirt, pretty blouse, fabulous necklace, and pink heels, all because I chose to accept the help. Don't be afraid to admit you need help and, most importantly, accept it! By saying yes and allowing someone to assist you, you'll get things done faster or better. Plus, the experience may just end up with you feeling like a million bucks!

Be thankful for the help. Gratitude is one of the keys to getting the help that you need. Say "thank you" always and often. Be grateful for the help that you receive. Acknowledge that what the person did for you was important and that it helped you. Write a handwritten card, order a thoughtful gift, send an email message, or even give a shout out on Facebook to let the person know how much you genuinely appreciated their time and help. When you say "thank you," you're actually telling the universe, "more of this please." The guidance and assistance you need will keep coming more and more as you consistently practice expressing your gratitude.

YOUR PIT CREW ROSTER

"You can do anything, but not everything."

~ Anonymous

As you prepare to enter the track to your success, you need to assemble your own pit crew. Get very specific about the kind of help you will need to achieve your goals and who the people are to fill those roles. Let's start recruiting!

Your pit crew roster should include:

1. You, the Driver
You are number one on the team roster! The person in the driver's seat has the most important role in this race. The driver needs specific skills and talents to drive the car around the track. As you sit in the driver's seat, you will need to bring your unique abilities to the achievement of your goals. Where do your talents lie? What are the things that you love to do? What are you going to contribute to your success?

Dan Sullivan, creator of the "Strategic Coach" program defines a unique ability as:

- A superior ability that other people notice and value
- Something you love doing and want to do as much as possible
- Energizing both for you and others
- A trait you keep getting better at while never running out of possibilities for further improvement

Take some time to make a list of the unique abilities you bring to the table regarding your goals. This activity will help you identify where you should spend most of your time while making it clear who you need to recruit for your team.

You should concentrate your effort on activities in alignment with your unique abilities and talents. All of the other items you're not good at or that you dislike should be delegated to someone else. Save yourself time and frustration by only focusing on your true talents.

2. Your Biggest Fans

Your loyal fans are the people who support you, encourage you, and most importantly, believe in you, even when you don't believe in yourself. Your fans will uplift you and encourage you with their positive outlook. They're your biggest cheerleaders and will cheer you on to your victory! They'll be the first to say, "I'm so excited for you. I can't wait to see you crush your goals." When you're having a bad day or when you're struggling with doubt, they'll be the ones who pick you up. Be selective about telling your goals and dreams to people who are positive and are going to support you. Stay away from any negative influences.

> **"I'm a success today because I had a friend who believed in me and I didn't have the heart to let him down."**
>
> ~ Abraham Lincoln

Right now you might be thinking, "Gosh, I don't have anyone in my life who is all that supportive of me. I'm embarrassed to share my goals with others. What if they shoot them down?" Again, remember that you get what you give. To find your biggest fans, start by being an enthusiastic supporter of others' goals. Be the encouraging voice to your closest friends, to your family members, and to your colleagues. Cheer them on and watch your supporters begin to appear.

Watch people light up as you say the following types of comments to them:

- "I'm so proud of you for wanting to start your own business. I believe you will be successful, and I can't wait to be your first customer!"

- "It's so exciting to hear that you're planning a trip to Europe! I know you will have a fabulous time, and it's going to be so much fun to hear all about it. Don't forget to take lots of pictures because I can't wait to see them!"

- "I never knew that you wanted to write a musical. Thanks for sharing your dreams with me. I know you will succeed, and I want to be sitting front and center on opening night to see your show."

When you begin using comments like these in your daily interactions with others, soon you're going to find encouraging words come right back to you. People will begin to reciprocate and ask you, "What are your dreams? Where do you want to go on vacation? I can't wait to hear about your new book." You'll start attracting those types of raving fans into your life and receive their support and encouragement. They'll be shouting your name and cheering for you as you inch closer and closer to the finish line!

3. Crew Chief

Set yourself up for success by naming your chief assistant, your right-hand person. It might be your spouse, friend, partner, team member, or co-worker. By having that person right by your side, it's going to accelerate your progress. If you're looking to buy that new home, it could be your spouse. If you're a business owner looking to launch a brand new service, it might be an executive assistant who is going to keep you organized, provide customer service, and take care of all the details behind the scenes for you. The crew chief is extremely involved throughout the entire process of achieving your goals, from initial planning right through to the Winner's Circle.

Keep these recommended traits in mind as you select this critical member of your team:

- **Supportive** - Remains in constant communication with you and fully supports you in this endeavor
- **Strategic** - Has the ability to plan, serve as an advisor, and keep you on track
- **Decisive** - Has the perspective to help you make decisions, sometimes quickly
- **Loyal** - Has earned your complete trust and is committed to helping you realize your success
- **Competent** - Has the knowledge and ability to help you achieve your goals
- **Hard-working** - Is not afraid to dig in and take action

4. Crew Members

Pit crew members keep working to get the car and the driver to the finish line. On the road to your success, they will be your daily helpers assisting with services to keep you moving along the track. Remember that you will be focused on tasks related to your unique abilities, and you need to delegate the things that are not in your wheelhouse. Now, you can't delegate everything, but identify what you don't enjoy doing or simply aren't good at doing. Then, give those tasks to somebody else who loves to do that kind of work or complete that sort of task.

During The Big Drive, I had a team of virtual assistants who worked hours and hours to configure the software, upload content for the marketing campaigns, and make sure the software was ready for the new customers. I also hired implementation coaches to help get new customers up and running on the new systems. They coached and trained each new customer to learn how to use the software and troubleshoot these programs. I couldn't have won that competition without my crew. They helped me manage the increased workload I experienced by selling such a large quantity in such a short time. I am extremely grateful for all of them and all of the hard work they put in to contribute to my success.

Let's say you have a revenue goal you want to hit or exceed. Start thinking about the kind of support you will need to achieve that goal. Look to your current staff and team members and share your mission with them. Maybe you'll need to hire some new talent who can help you innovate, sell more, or provide additional service. If you are looking to move into your new home, your crew members might be the movers that help you pack and move your belongings. Or, they may be cleaners who work to tidy up your previous home and prepare the new home for your arrival.

Get your crew members in place to help with the daily grind and to solve problems on the road to your victory. You will move along faster by having a solid team behind you.

5. Experts, Mechanics, and Technicians

These experts will be masters in techniques, skills, or crafts that will assist you in achieving your goals. They are going to help you reduce your learning curve and help you get things done faster and better. Sometimes you just need to let things go and search for the expert who can assist you.

It could be a technician who has the computer programming skills and knowledge that you have no desire to ever learn, but could help you achieve your goals. You might seek a financial advisor for expert advice to find out, "How can I budget better?" or "How can I strategize this so that we can increase our revenue?" If you're planning your dream vacation, the expert might be a travel agent. This pro is going to know the best time of year to go so that you don't end up taking a cruise in the middle of hurricane season that just ruins your vacation entirely! Do you have fitness goals? An expert that you could find would be a personal trainer, somebody who is going to know the best exercises for you and recommend a diet that's going to help you reach your ideal body weight. You can pull in experts if you're looking to do some rebranding. You might need a graphic designer to help you pick out the right colors, select the right pictures, and create that wireframe for your website. Look for these experts so you're not doing it all by yourself.

During The Big Drive, I sought out many experts to help me develop my new programs. I had copywriters, graphic designers, and marketing specialists who were brought in to share their knowledge with me and move my product in the direction it needed to go. I'm never afraid or too proud to find people who can contribute to my projects and help me achieve new levels of success. Some may think that asking for help is a sign of weakness, but I disagree. Asking for help is one of the smartest things you can do! Leveraging other people's talents will accelerate your success.

6. Motivators

Finally, gather your motivators. Going after your goals is a trans-formative experience, and you'll need people who are going to encourage you and support you in a different role than your biggest fans do. Your motivators have the skills and knowledge to guide you in the right direction, overcome your obstacles, and reach the next level of success.

Here are the key motivators to look for:

- **Coaches -** Hiring a coach, even for a short period of time, will help accelerate your success. Whether it's a business, life, spiritual, or health coach, he or she will provide you with fresh insight and inspiration. Look for a coach you can be open and honest with to guide your transformation while encouraging you and keeping you on track. Maybe that person has a special expertise or previous experience that will guide you through the process of achieving your goals. Seek advice from your coach when you feel stuck. He or she can give you direction by providing a perspective to allow you to move forward, identify blind spots and lessons, and help you avoid or bypass obstacles.

- **Teachers and Leaders -** Seek out teachers and leaders in your industry who can help you learn and grow. Look to enroll in local classes, register for online courses, or attend conferences and workshops to further develop your skills. Teachers can also be authors of books or other programs who will give you the skills and direction you need specifically related to your goals. Always continue to learn and grow. Constantly acquire the skills and knowledge you need to develop your unique abilities and further your success.

- **Mentors -** Some of my favorite motivators are my mentors. In her book, *Escape from Cubicle Nation*, Pamela Slim encourages readers to assemble what she calls your "High Council of Jedi Knights." This council comprises people you respect and admire, your role models. They can be people you know personally. Or, they can be well-known experts you want to emulate and who make you feel inspired to achieve more. Also, look to find somebody you can work with one-on-one, who will mentor you and guide you to your success. Choose mentors you admire and who will share wisdom that will help you achieve new levels of success. Your mentor will teach you from experience and will support you to become the person you want to be.

- **Mastermind Group** - Another great motivator is being part of a mastermind group. A mastermind is a group of like-minded people with similar interests and skill levels who get together regularly for peer brainstorming, to provide feedback, and give each other support. My husband and I belong to a business mastermind, and we meet once a month with about seven other business owners. Since joining a mastermind, I've grown exponentially, personally and professionally. During our meetings, we share things that we're currently doing in our businesses and get feedback from other members of the group. The members also keep you accountable to your growth each month and share resources and ideas with you. If you can't find a mastermind in your area, create your own! Plan to meet up regularly to work on your goals together.

FILLING THE ROLES

"I can do things you cannot, you can do things I cannot, together we can do great things."

~ Mother Teresa

Since you now realize that you don't create alone and that you have many roles that need to be filled in order to help guide you to your victory, you might be worried that you don't have everyone in place yet. With the combination of a little bit of work, some faith, and being open and receptive, you can find the right people.

Here are a few tips for finding people to fill those vacancies:

1. **Assess what you already have.** To get started, it's a good idea to think about who you already have in your life that can support you. Create a team roster by listing the roles that you will need to fill in order to achieve your goals: crew chief, fans, helpers, technicians, coaches, etc.

   After you write down your team roster, take some time to assess the support you already have. First, think about the people who are there to assist you right now. Fill in the names of the people already in your life who are fulfilling those roles. You will find that this is an easy task. Next, quickly reach out to the people on your mind who can assist you and ask them for their support. You will then see the vacant roles, the ones you still need to fill. Place a question mark by those roles, and begin the search for your new team members.

2. **Make a "Mary Poppins List."** For the vacancies on your list, I suggest you make what I call, a "Mary Poppins List." In the Disney movie *Mary Poppins* the two children, Jane and Michael, had a really bad history of chasing their nannies away by misbehaving and scaring them. The children were in search of the perfect nanny. After taking some time to write a letter, a job description, for their perfect nanny, Jane and Michael presented their mother and father with their "advertisement." It was their description of the perfect nanny they had been hoping to have.

   Here is their letter:

   > *Wanted a nanny for two adorable children,*
   > *If you want this choice position*
   > *Have a cheery disposition*
   > *Rosy cheeks, no warts*
   > *Play games, all sorts*
   >
   > *You must be kind, you must be witty*
   > *Very sweet and fairly pretty*
   > *Take us on outings, give us treats*
   > *Sing songs, bring sweets*

Never be cross or cruel
Never give us Castor oil or gruel
Love us as a son and daughter
And never smell of barley water

If you won't scold and dominate us
We will never give you cause to hate us
We won't hide your spectacles, so you can't see
Put toads in your bed or pepper in your tea

Hurry nanny, many thanks

Sincerely, Jane and Michael Banks

After the children sang this description aloud in song to their parents, the father hastily took their letter and in disbelief said that it was "nonsense." He tore up the letter and threw the paper pieces into the fireplace. The pieces of paper magically flew up through the chimney and into the sky, where Mary Poppins was sitting on a cloud. She received and read the children's letter, and immediately prepared to answer the request because she fit the description perfectly. Soon, she arrived at their home and assumed her position as the nanny that they had been wishing for.

You too, can create your "Mary Poppins List" and write a description of the exact person you wish to bring into your life. By writing a very specific list of the qualities you are searching for, you will attract that perfect person into your life. By completing this activity, you are sending a message into the universe about exactly want you want.

3. **Be patient and be open to guidance.** You have this specific list of the people you need and the description of the roles they will fill. It's time to have a little patience while you wait for that help to come to you. Think about it as if you are growing a garden. You've just planted the seeds of your desires to find the help that you need. You know that you don't plant seeds in the garden one day and expect a fully grown plant after only 10 minutes. Be patient and wait for the universe to grow the seeds for you. You've written your

list. It's out in the universe now. Help is on the way and will come to you at the perfect time.

Be receptive to the help and guidance that will present itself to you in many forms. You might meet somebody and strike up a conversation that leads you to a solution. You might come across a person on Facebook, at an event, or in a store who has that skill or knows somebody who has that skill. It might be something you read in a magazine or online. An idea could just pop into your head! Be open to that guidance. Take it as a message from the universe, seek more information, and act on it.

By assembling your team, you will feel empowered and will be equipped to head out on your journey. Can you hear the cheers from the stands, and see the smiles from your team? The start of the race is getting closer and there are only a few more things you need to do to prepare.

 ## GET INTO GEAR

- Understand that many people work together to achieve goals.

- Be open to asking for help, receiving the support, and expressing gratitude each day.

- Identify your unique abilities and determine the tasks you need to delegate to others.

- Fill the roles you need by identifying your crew chief, crew members, experts, and motivators to help guide you to your success.

- Be patient and open to guidance when filling these supportive roles that will guide you to success.

 ## ACCELERATE TOWARD YOUR SUCCESS

1. Recognize the unique abilities that you can bring to each goal by making a list of your skills and talents. What do you bring to the table? What are your gifts and strengths? What do you love to do? This will be the starting point of knowing where to ask for help.

2. Start to gain support by creating a team roster for each goal. Make a list of your biggest fans, crew chief, crew members, experts, and motivators who will assist you along your journey. Reach out to the people in your inner circle who can get on board to help you. This activity will help you see the roles that will need to be filled, and you can begin to seek out the support required to make your goals your reality.

ON THE ROAD REFLECTIONS

In your journal, write a "Mary Poppins List" for a role you need to fill. On the top of the paper, write the position. Begin by writing a description of the role. Then, get very specific about the qualities, skills, and talents you desire in this person. Release your list into the world and begin to watch for this person to appear in your life.

We don't create alone.
Recognize the help that you need, ask for help,
and be willing to receive the help.

CHAPTER

THINK LIKE A CHAMPION

> "Our subconscious minds have no sense of humor, play
> no jokes and cannot tell the difference between reality
> and an imagined thought or image. What we continually
> think about eventually will manifest in our lives."
>
> ~ Robert Collier

As we move into the next phase on your journey to sweet success, give yourself a pat on the back for all of the hard work you have put into building a solid foundation. You have a clear destination now that you've identified your specific goals. You have worked to maintain a state of belief regarding your success. And, you have rounded up the support that you need to succeed. Congratulations! Now, the next leg of your trip is all about focus and using your thoughts and spoken words to get even clearer about what your success will look like. Every step you take will bring your success more into focus. It's time to think like a champion and learn how to carefully choose the right words to think and say because they are going to impact your mindset, your actions, and ultimately your results.

SHIFTING GEARS

I came into The Big Drive contest realizing I had this runner-up, second-place mentality about myself. As I reflected back on my life, I realized that I never took first place or won the grand prize in any contest or competition. In my elementary years, I was an organist and entered regional contests where I would play a musical piece competing against others in my age group and experience level. Over the years, I proudly came home with the third place trophy several times and the second place trophy occasionally. I treasured those symbols of my hard work, but I yearned for the first place trophy. I wanted to feel the pride and satisfaction of setting it on my shelf to be displayed with all of my other achievements. I recalled other events and competitions similar to the organ contests. Again, I was often good enough to be among the top competitors. However, the results always placed me as the runner-up. The coveted grand prize continued to elude me.

Coming in as a runner-up in Infusionsoft's Ultimate Marketer contest was a turning point for me. I remember arriving at that conference in March 2011 with high hopes and big dreams to walk away with the title of "Ultimate Marketer." I worked so hard and had this incredible desire to inspire the attendees, the other small business owners there. In fact, I had been working through a program to help me apply the law of attraction to manifest this experience. But, as soon as I saw my competition, Jermaine Griggs from Hear and Play Music; and Sean Kelly and Andy Mackensen from HUMAN Healthy Vending, I immediately took note of my limitations and their phenomenal skills as marketers. Then, the negative, second-place thoughts bombarded my head like an avalanche:

> *"Wow! These guys are amazing. I don't feel like I even belong here."*

> *"How could I even compete with such amazing, brilliant marketers?"*

> *"Why was I even selected as a finalist? They are much more experienced and more successful than me."*

Guess what? I left InfusionCon that year as a runner-up, my head hanging low and my spirits crushed. I asked myself, "How could this have happened?" I felt embarrassed. I felt like a failure and the laughing stock of the entire event. What I didn't realize at that point was that I WAS already a winner. I also didn't realize that I had achieved an amazing accomplishment that would launch my career as a sales and marketing consultant. In fact, I had achieved exactly what my thoughts and words had been saying all along. I told myself I was good enough to be one of the top three finalists, but I also told myself that I wasn't good enough to come home with the grand prize. The universe had brought to me exactly what I had ordered. Acknowledging this about myself and being able to overcome it was key to winning The Big Drive.

During The Big Drive contest, I became very aware of the thoughts I was thinking and the words I was saying. I knew there was something about the way my brain thought that I needed to change. Making that change in my thought process would allow me to become that first place winner. It was not going to be easy for me. There was a lot of hard work ahead of me, because I had years of second-place programming to unravel. I grew up worrying a lot, having anxiety about things, and often assuming the worst about situations. Once I identified this as a problem, I made a huge, concerted effort to change my mindset. I asked myself, "What can I do to change these thoughts and replace them with more positive statements?" I searched for simple, yet effective methods to retrain my brain into thinking like a champion. I worked daily to reprogram these old thoughts, which were deeply ingrained in my subconscious mind.

I started to practice a nightly meditation, a track with ocean waves I listened to with headphones while I fell asleep. Within these ocean waves were subliminal messages. Even though I couldn't hear them, they told me positive messages about myself:

"All that I seek is seeking me."

"I receive all the help that I need."

"I am a success."

"I've got what it takes to win."

Instead of worrying about losing the contest or stressing about all the things I had to get done the next day, these empowering statements were repeated to me in my ear as I fell asleep every night. The most important thoughts that we think are the thoughts we are thinking while we fall asleep. They are the thoughts that stay with us all night long as we rest and dream.

I decided it would also be helpful for me to have positive messages I could read every day. Infusionsoft, the sales and marketing automation software I work with, has the ability to create a sequence that automatically sends out daily emails to prospects or customers. I thought, "What if I created a campaign that sent me emails with the same positive messages I listened to every night during my meditations?" I got to work and created a series of emails to be sent to my inbox every morning. Each day I received an email with a positive message. When I checked my email each morning, the first thing I saw in my inbox was a message from me, saying "I am a winner," "I am a success," "I've got what it takes to win." I would read it aloud or close my eyes and internalize the message. I still receive these emails to this day, and so do my friends and clients!

I also understood that I needed to start saying positive things to myself. Instead of saying, "Oh, you'll never win," "It's too hard," and "You've never sold this much before," I turned it around. I started saying positive affirmations, my "I Am" statements. I would say, throughout the day, "I am a success," "I am a first place winner," "I am an inspiration to others," and I made it a daily habit. I wrote them down, thought about them, and spoke them aloud to myself and others. My tendency toward negative thoughts was being overcome with good, positive thoughts that would propel me to my victory.

WE CREATE IN THREE WAYS

> **"You only have control over three things in your life. Number one, the thoughts you think. Number two, the images you visualize. And number three, the actions you take, your behavior. And how you use these three things determines everything you experience."**
>
> ~ Jack Canfield

We apply the same three principles in everything that we do, from something as small as a dinner, to something as big as winning a car. Just as Jack Canfield said in his quote, what we create is based on three things we have control over:

1. The thoughts we think
2. The pictures we imagine
3. The actions we take

One night I was planning what to make my family for dinner. I asked myself, "What can we have for dinner?" I had some ideas and thoughts beginning to float around in my mind - meatloaf, tacos, grilled cheese sandwiches. Bingo! Grilled cheese and tomato soup sounded really good! I began to imagine more clearly what that meal would look like. I could see the hot sandwiches and steaming soup placed at each seat at the table. I imagined a bowl of fresh cut fruit and another bowl filled with carrots. Most importantly, I saw the smiling faces of a happy husband and happy kids. This was a meal we could all agree on! I also imagined how a hot meal would feel during the winter evening and how delicious that sandwich would taste. My stomach started growling at this point, so I went to the store and purchased the bread, cheese, soup, and other items I needed to prepare the dinner. That evening I prepped our family meal, and we sat down to enjoy it together as a family. You see, I THOUGHT about what I wanted for dinner and then I started to IMAGINE the pictures of what dinner would look like. Finally, I took ACTION by shopping for the food and preparing the dinner—a simple example of how your thoughts, images, and actions can bring something into being.

I also used my thoughts, my images, and my actions to create a not so pleasant experience—a foreclosure. A few years back, times were tough. Our business suffered during the economic collapse, and I started thinking about how we were going to manage the mortgage payments and all the other debts we had incurred from our business and medical expenses. Then I started wondering, "What if we lost our house? Where would we go? Where would we live? What would my neighbors think?" I started feeling embarrassed that we would be forced to leave our house and that our family, friends, and neighbors would judge us for that. I also imagined having to pack up my house and leave with our neighbors snickering or feeling pity for our family. The actions that I took were right along with our pending doom, by telling the bank we had no way out and even looking for rental properties online.

I prepared for that imminent foreclosure with the words I spoke, the pictures I imagined in my mind, and the actions I took each day. And, so it came to be. Not my proudest moment, but one that I can now accept 100% responsibility for and reflect on for its growth opportunity.

We have to be careful because we're always creating, everything in our lives—everything—every day. Champions understand we're always creating in three ways: through our thoughts, our images, and our actions. In this chapter, we'll focus on how you create with your thoughts and words.

YOUR THOUGHTS ARE THINGS AND YOUR WORDS ARE POWERFUL

Studies in quantum physics are proving that our thoughts are things. Dr. Masaru Emoto conducted groundbreaking research that demonstrated how words and sounds have an effect on the molecular structure of water. He experimented by exposing water to words or music, froze the water, and then examined it under a microscope. The research team examined the patterns of the crystals in the ice and took photographs. What was really interesting is that when they started to look, they could see that certain thoughts, words, and experiences would make the water look different, very different based on the positivity or negativity of a particular sound.

The water that had been exposed to the lovely song "Imagine" by John Lennon, had water crystals arranged in symmetrical designs resembling a beautiful white snowflake. Conversely, the water that had been exposed to heavy metal music appeared much different when Dr. Emoto looked at it under the microscope. It was dark, had no particular patterns, and looked, well, ugly! During additional experiments, specific words were spoken to the water repeatedly. The water being spoken to with the words "love" and "gratitude" also had beautiful hexagonal crystals while the water that was told 'you disgust me' and 'you're disgusting' did not contain any beauty at all! How interesting to discover that those words and songs had such an impact on transforming the molecular structure of the water. (You can see the photographs from Dr. Emoto's research by doing a quick Google search.)

Dr. Emoto also did similar experiments with rice and came to the same conclusion. So, your aunt ISN'T crazy for talking and singing to her plants to help them thrive. If water, rice, and plants can be changed so drastically by the words spoken to them, imagine what's happening to every cell in our body based on the thoughts we say to ourselves! Remember, what you think about, you bring about. It's critical that you're thinking the right things and saying the right words.

Along the same lines, my friend and client, Thomas, shared a story from www.marrscoaching.com that also demonstrates how our thoughts and words are so powerful.

This is the story of two travelers and a farmer:

> A traveler came upon an old farmer hoeing in his field beside the road. Eager to rest his feet, the wanderer hailed the countryman, who seemed happy enough to straighten his back and talk for a moment.
>
> "What sort of people live in the next town?" asked the stranger.
>
> "What were the people like where you've come from?" replied the farmer, answering the question with another question.
>
> "They were a bad lot, troublemakers all, and lazy too. The most selfish people in the world and not a one of them to be trusted. I'm happy to be leaving those scoundrels."
>
> "Is that so," replied the old farmer. "Well, I'm afraid you'll find the same sort in the next town."
>
> Disappointed, the traveler trudged on his way and the farmer returned to his work.
>
> Sometime later another stranger, coming from the same direction, hailed the farmer, and they stopped to talk.
>
> "What sort of people live in the next town?" he asked.

"What were the people like where you've come from?" replied the farmer once again.

"They were the best people in the world, hard-working, honest, and friendly. I'm sorry to be leaving them."

"Fear not," said the farmer. "You'll find the same sort in the next town."

Thomas and I had a great conversation about the message of this story and discussed how what we focus on is what we're going to get more of in our life. The lesson of this story is to remember that you get what you're looking for, and the things that you say, the things that you focus on, are what you're going to bring into your life. Remember, you get what you give. If you're giving off negative thoughts you're going to get more negativity in your life. If you're giving positive thoughts, you're going to receive more positivity in your life.

What do you focus on in any given situation? Are you pointing out the bad or focusing on the negative in most situations? Or are you really grateful for the positives that you experience? Because again, you are going to get what you give. What you think about, you bring about, and what you focus on will continue to manifest in your life.

UNDERSTANDING YOUR SUBCONSCIOUS MIND

"Whatever we plant in our subconscious mind and nourish with repetition and emotion will one day become a reality."

~ Earl Nightingale

Your subconscious mind holds the power to bring what you desire into your life. You know your thoughts are things; they have an impact on your reality and the experience you want to create in your life. Your subconscious mind is there to actually agree with you. Yes, to agree with you! It's much like at a drive-through. You get what you order. If you go through the drive-through and order a Big Mac, fries, and a Coke, you're not going to get a filet-o-fish and an apple pie. It's the same thing with your subconscious mind. Whatever you're telling it, whatever it's hearing, is what you're going to get.

Your subconscious mind has been programmed with thoughts and beliefs throughout your entire life. These influences come from sources that you have no control over. In some cases, you might not even realize what has been impacting you: the media, how your parents raised you, what you were taught in school. All of these influences have programmed your mind with thoughts and beliefs. Let me share a story that conveys this point. It's about a woman who discovers why, for years, she's been cutting the end off of her dinner ham before baking it.

> A daughter was watching her mother prepare a ham for dinner and noticed that she cut off the end of the ham before placing it in the pan and into the oven.
>
> The daughter inquisitively asked, "Mommy, why did you just cut off the end of the ham?"
>
> The mother replied, "I don't know, it's just how my mother always made the ham. She cut the end off before she put it in the pan. That's how she'd make it and it always turned out delicious, so that's how I make it!"
>
> So the next time this woman saw her mother she asked her, "Mom, I was wondering, why do you cut off the end of the ham as you're preparing it?" The Mom replied, "Well, that's what Grandma always did, so that's how I bake my ham. Grandma always cooked a perfect ham!"
>
> The next time they saw Grandma, they asked her, "Grandma, why do you cut off the end of the ham?" Grandma's response was, "Well, because my pan was really small, and I had to cut the end off to make it fit."

Imagine finding out you'd been cutting off the end of the ham for years and find out the reason why is really no reason at all! Doesn't it make you wonder what behaviors are ingrained in your daily life for no good reason? What are you doing that you don't know the root reason for why? What you think or do simply because those thoughts and beliefs have been programmed in your subconscious mind throughout your entire life? The good news is that your subconscious mind can be changed and redirected. It is there to help you by agreeing with you 100% of the time so let's begin to use it in your favor more of the time!

Here are some easy ways to change and redirect the thoughts programmed in your subconscious mind:

1. **Be aware.** The most important way to make changes to your thought process is to become super aware of the thoughts you think and the words you speak. I always say the number one catalyst for change is acknowledgment of the issue or problem. Once you are aware of things that need to change, you can get to work! It can be scary to realize the full power of your thoughts at first, but don't be afraid. When you begin to note all of the negative things you've been saying to yourself day after day, you can simply start making changes, one thought at a time. Soon the number of positive thoughts will exceed the number of negative thoughts and you'll begin to notice a difference in what you experience in your life. You will find you are happier and new ideas and opportunities will drop into your lap that will bring you closer to your goals.

2. **Be clear and direct.** You can also talk to your subconscious to tell it exactly what you want it to do. Remember to give it clear and direct commands. Think of it as though you're talking to a 3-year-old child. You're not going to give a lengthy, detailed explanation to a toddler, such as "This toy on the floor needs to be picked up. You should really be picking up the toy and putting it over in the box because we don't want to trip over it. We don't want to fall and get hurt, and we want our house to look nice in case somebody stops by unexpectedly...." Instead, you're going to be very clear, concise, and direct and tell the 3-year-old, "Pick up the toy and put it in the box." When negative thoughts begin to swirl around in your head, tell yourself exactly what you want and repeat it. During The Big Drive, I kept telling

myself, "I'm going to win. I will come home with the grand prize." Simple and to the point commands began to shift my thinking to that of a champion, and it can help you, too!

3. **Be bold.** When you begin to consciously think more positively, you may have some bad ones sneak in once in a while. It's OK! Just tell the negative thoughts to "Go away!" Each time it comes back, say it again. "Go away!" Eventually, it will get the picture and leave your mind. I use this strategy every time an annoying song gets stuck in my head, replaying over and over again in my mind. When I get tired of the song, I tell my subconscious mind, "No, I don't want to hear it anymore." It might take a few tries, but eventually that song does in fact go away. You can do the same thing with your negative thoughts. Simply tell your subconscious mind and that pesky thought what you think of it. Here are some handy go-to phrases:

   ▪ "No, go away."

   ▪ "Delete."

   ▪ "Cancel that thought."

Even better, say, "no" and replace it with a positive thought. Take control of your thoughts by empowering yourself with these bold and simple phrases.

4. **Be consistent.** Be careful not to give your subconscious mind mixed messages. You can't tell it, "Yes, this is going to happen" one minute and then say, "No it's not" the next. Since your subconscious mind is there to agree with you, it's important to be consistent. For example, you may be thinking, "I'd love to start my own business," and your subconscious mind agrees with you and repeats, "Yes, you'd love to start your own business." Then you think, "But starting a business is hard," and your subconscious mind says, "Yes, starting a business is hard." Your next thought might be, "I would love the freedom of being my own boss." Your subconscious mind agrees with you, "Yes, you would love the freedom of being your own boss." However, if your next thought is, "But I don't have enough money to get this started," your subconscious mind will agree with you, "Yeah, you don't

have enough money to get this started." Alternating positives and negatives will keep you going around and around in circles never getting anywhere! Continuously sending the same positive messages over and over again will keep you directly on the path to achieving your goals.

Use your subconscious mind to your advantage by being aware of your thoughts and being clear, direct, and consistent when working with it. In no time, you'll see how easy it is to redirect to more positive thinking and get your subconscious to work in your favor.

RETRAIN YOUR BRAIN

You know that you have a great tool—your subconscious mind—but you also know it's been programmed, maybe programmed the wrong way in some cases. It's time to retrain that brain! Retraining takes effort, but it can be fun and easy if you bring the right attitude. Here are some strategies that can help you start retraining your brain into thinking more positively so that you're bringing more positive experiences into your life:

1. **Choose a mantra.** To begin the process of retraining your brain, I invite you to choose a mantra. A mantra is a statement or slogan that is repeated frequently. During The Big Drive, the mantra for my team was, "We got this!" It started when I met with my team of virtual assistants at my home office to begin their training of the software and systems they would configure. We were getting excited about our upcoming projects, slapped some high fives with each other, and someone shouted, "We got this!" It stuck and became our mantra to pep us up in the midst of the hard work and obstacles we faced.

   Your mantra should be simple, catchy, and fun to say! Capture your own personality in your new slogan. It should feel natural to say and should bring a smile to your face, too. To get ideas for your mantra, take a look at these possibilities:

   - Piece of cake!
   - We're simply the best!

- My time has come. My time is now.
- Success is within my reach!
- Never give up!
- It's my time to shine!

Once you've selected your mantra, have fun displaying it! Share it with your team and make it your "go-to" slogan. Order colorful t-shirts with the phrase. Have coffee mugs made. Print it out on fancy paper, frame it, and have it next to your workspace or on your bathroom mirror so you remember to say that mantra over and over again. You might even notice the phrase starts showing up all around you on signs, posters, Facebook shares, and knick-knacks at the store. Snap photos when you see it and buy those trinkets to surround yourself with these motivational reminders. Your mantra will help you think positively throughout the day and will inspire your team and/or supporters!

2. **Practice meditation.** Meditating is a great way to clear your mind of the negative thoughts and the mindless chatter in your brain. It helps you make time to quiet the noise. Try taking just a few minutes every day to get centered and silent. There's so much information being thrown at you day in and day out. You're juggling home, work, relationships and fun, too. With so many thoughts creeping in and out of our mind all day, it's important to take the time to get quiet.

To begin meditating, find a place where you can sit comfortably, maybe on the floor or in a chair, and quietly play a calming piece of music. Then, begin to breathe in and out. Focus on your breath as you breathe in and as you exhale. During that time, just clear your mind of any thoughts. If a thought comes in, tell it to go away. With meditation, you want to just sit there and enjoy the quiet. It's a really great way to get rid of those negative thoughts. When I first started meditating, I couldn't help but have my mind wander a bit and begin to chatter again. Don't be too hard on yourself if you experience the same thing.

I have found that using some resources has been helpful for me. Give these a try if you are wondering where to begin or want something new to add to your meditation routine:

- A simple YouTube search will bring up a variety of meditations that you can listen to while you take a break from work or when you need some quiet time at home.

- Kelly Howell has created some fantastic downloads available at **www.brainsync.com**. The one I listened to daily throughout The Big Drive is called "Create Success," which is a subliminal reprogramming track.

- There is also another program called HoloSync, which is at **www.centerpoint.com**. It's a really great meditation that quiets my mind and helps me relax and fall asleep.

- One of my clients recently showed me a convenient phone app she started using call Buddhify. Get it at **www.buddhify.com** and take it with you anywhere to experience a guided mental break. The app even offers a variety of meditation topics such as taking a work break, having trouble sleeping, and feeling stressed out. It's a meditation in the palm of your hand!

3. **Repeat positive affirmations.** You can also say positive affirmations. Positive affirmations remind me of the quirky Stuart Smalley from *Saturday Night Live* who said, "I'm good enough, I'm smart enough, and doggone it, people like me." It was a funny sketch, but it's so true in a practical way. Repeating powerful affirmations will empower you to remember your strengths and unique abilities.

Here are some examples of positive affirmations:

- I am a smart and successful business person.
- I am a talented writer.
- I am creative.
- I am resourceful.

- I am an inspiration to others.
- I am a leader.
- I am a winner.

If you have trouble writing your "I Am" statements, just go back to your unique abilities that we talked about in Chapter 3. What qualities, skills, or talents do you bring to the table regarding your goals? Write those down because you ARE amazing, you ARE awesome, you ARE gifted, and you ARE talented. It's my wish that throughout this journey you become a better you, more of who you already are.

When negative thoughts pop in, repeat your "I Am" statements. It's a great way to help you feel better. I suggest writing a list of your statements on index cards, on paper slips, or in your journal. Post them where you can look at them daily. When you see them, repeat them aloud. Display reminders around you that are going to inspire you and keep you thinking positively. Make it a habit to say your affirmations daily. Maybe it's the first thing you do when you wake up in the morning, while you're showering, on your drive home, or walking your dog. When you commit to repeating them daily, you're going to see some powerful transformations, and you'll have more confidence in your ability to achieve your goals.

4. **Share a positive focus.** This is sharing something positive with others regarding your work, your business, or your personal life. Our family begins our dinners with a positive focus. We go around the table and everybody takes a turn telling something wonderful that happened to them during the day. Whenever I host my online group coaching calls, I invite the attendees to share something positive in the chat box. It gets everything started on a better note.

You can practice this with your team at work as you get started with your workday, at the beginning of a meeting, or even at the start of a conversation. Invite others to share an experience or something that's been going really well and then share yours, too. Maybe it's that you're really proud of your kids for the grades on their report card, or your team really pulled through last week with hitting the metrics that you gave them. Whether it's with a group of people or a one-on-one conversation, give it a try! You'll see the energy level rise, which will guide the experience into a positive one.

GET INTO GEAR

- We create in three ways, through our thoughts, our images, and our actions.

- We need to remember that our thoughts are things that will enter into our lives so we must make a concerted effort to keep them positive.

- Our subconscious mind is there to agree with us no matter what we're thinking, both positive and negative.

- We can retrain our subconscious mind into thinking more positively using strategies discussed in this chapter.

ACCELERATE TOWARD YOUR SUCCESS –

1. Write 5–10 "I Am" statements. These statements are extremely powerful in helping you stay positive throughout the day. "I am a winner. I am an inspiration to others. I am successful. I am a talented musician." Keep them handy by writing them on index cards or printing them on paper. Read them throughout the day to feel empowered.

2. Choose your mantra, your slogan or saying that you can repeat often to maintain a positive attitude. Write it on a post-it and place it in your workspace or on your bathroom mirror. Read it, say it aloud, and mean it!

ON THE ROAD REFLECTIONS

What is your positive focus today? Write about the wonderful things that have happened to you today, this week, or this month that make you feel wonderful. What do you have to be grateful for? Have you received great news? When you intentionally think about the blessings in your life, you can't help but think and feel positive about your life.

You must be aware that you're always creating. Everything in your life is created by your thoughts, images, and actions.

CHAPTER

SEE THE CHECKERED FLAG

"Logic will get you from A to B. Imagination will
take you everywhere."

~ Albert Einstein

You're well on your way! You've clearly identified your goals. You've worked hard to achieve and maintain a state of belief that you can get it done. You've assembled the important people who will help you along the road. And you've been retraining your brain to think positively so you can begin to attract the right people, ideas, and opportunities into your life. Now it's time you for to start envisioning the checkered flag, the symbol of your victory and the sign of your goal achievement. When you begin to actually see the images of your celebration in your mind, you will start to witness surprises manifesting in your life. Hold on to the wheel, aim high in your steering, and feel the excitement building as you focus on what your goal achievement will look like, sound like, and feel like.

VISUALIZING MY VICTORY

I closed my eyes as my head hit the pillow, and I snuggled into the blankets with my headphones placed over my ears. The relaxing sound of ocean waves began to soothe me from the hectic day. I began to imagine entering the banquet room filled with tables. I could hear laughter, voices, and the clanking of silverware hitting the plates. This celebration dinner was just like I remembered from the year before, although this time would be much more special to me. This time I would be sitting down with my family to enjoy the evening and to celebrate with the people who mattered most to me.

We enjoyed the meal together while the excitement began to stir inside of me. It felt like 1,000 butterflies were fluttering around my entire body. I had a special surprise tonight, and I couldn't wait to share the news with everyone at the event. After dinner, which I hardly touched due to the pure excitement I felt and my desire to get on with the program, the emcee finally walked up on stage and said it was time to acknowledge some very special people. He began to call the names of the top sales winners for The Big Drive contest. The third place winner was announced, and he walked onto the stage while the audience clapped and whistled. Then, the second place winner was called and handed a trophy, too. Then, it came time for the big announcement. My heart started beating faster with excitement, and I was full of pride. I imagined hearing my name being called, "And the grand prize winner of The Big Drive 2013 and the recipient of a brand-new Camaro is... Janette Gleason!"

I could hear the audience clapping loudly for me and cheering while I stood up to share the joy with my family. I hugged my husband and kissed my kids as I made my way up to the stage. The presenter said, "Congratulations, Janette, the car is yours!" and handed the car keys to me. I could see the entire staff on stage and everyone around me beaming with pride because of my ac-complishment. I said, "Thank you so much, can I please have a moment? I'd like to say a few words to the audience." I stepped up to the microphone, looked out at the sea of faces and could even spot some of my dear friends smiling and clapping for me. I imagined that I was overflowing with gratitude as I began my speech, and I started by thanking Infusionsoft for this opportunity and told everyone it was my wish to acknowledge the many people who helped me achieve this goal. I imagined announcing how excited I was and inviting my family up on stage. My husband and our children made their way up the steps to stand right by my side. I looked out at the room filled with my colleagues, my family, and the staff hosting the event.

"Thank you so much for this award. It is my greatest pleasure to introduce the two most important things in my life to each other tonight; my family and Infusionsoft." I introduced my husband, Joe, and our three children: Joey, Jianna, and Jillian. The kids loved the attention and applause, smiling from ear to ear with pride. Then, I turned to my kids and said, "If you want to be successful, you need to surround yourself with successful people. I want to introduce you to some very successful people." I waved my arm across the audience and said, "These are my friends from Infusionsoft. They are some of the smartest and brightest people in the world. They are there for me whenever I need help and are some of my best friends in the world."

Next, I had the pleasure of introducing my other special guests, my other family members and mentors. "Thank you for coming and sharing this special night with me, I love you all. Now I want to thank my team. I couldn't have achieved this without you." I called out their names individually and waved to them in the audience. "Last, I'd like to invite somebody very special to this stage--my Infusionsoft sales rep and partner, Cory Bendixen." The audience cheered and clapped as he made his way to my side up on the stage. I looked directly at him while I thanked him for helping me and encouraging me throughout this competition. I pulled out a trophy from the gift bag I had hidden on the floor and said, "Cory, I present you with this trophy for being my MVP. Thank you for everything." We hugged and then I turned one last time to the audience and I said my last 'thank you' to the group, while nodding my head and placing my hand on my heart.

Now, my visualization wasn't that detailed from the beginning, but each time I visualized that Celebratory Moment, it became more focused and more wonderful in my mind. You see, my victory wasn't just about winning the car but rather creating this amazing experience filled with love, pride, and gratitude. That was my true heart's desire. The car was a nice, extra bonus for me, the cherry on top! Amazing things began to happen as I visualized and imagined that movie playing over and over in my head every night as I fell asleep. I was presented with opportunities out of nowhere. I had no idea these would come to me. I found in myself a strength I didn't know I had. I showed up to sales calls with this confidence and this power that, again, I didn't know I had in me. I had ideas that would come to me as well. And, I visualized my

Celebratory Moment more than 100 times in my mind before it actually came true.

PICTURES BRING A CLEARER FOCUS

Holding images of success in your mind is a powerful tool for helping you achieve your goals. Remember that you create with images, that what you think about, you bring about. Along with the words you choose, pictures bring a much clearer focus about your goal achievement. It's time to strengthen your imagination muscles and actually begin to see that checkered flag in your mind's eye, to see in more detail what the experience of accomplishing your goals will look like.

Just imagine you're a race car driver with your sights set on winning the championship race. You close your eyes, relax, and intentionally focus on seeing a checkered flag in your mind. As you begin to imagine the flag more clearly, you see the pattern of black and white squares that will signal the completion of the race. You can actually see each individual fiber in the cloth weaving itself among the others. You hear the flag flapping in the wind and notice the massive crowd around you applauding, whistling, and cheering you on. You feel the adrenaline coursing through your veins, which gives you that extra push and propels you to the end of the race. You imagine the sense of pride you feel as you clearly see that flag inching closer and closer to you. And finally, you can actually taste your sweet victory as you whoosh right by that checkered flag and cross the finish line. Next, you enter the Winner's Circle where your friends and family are waiting all smiles to hug you, give you high fives, celebrate your success, and share the joy with you.

> **"Develop your imagination, you can use it to create in your mind what you hope to create in your life."**
>
> ~ Steven Covey

This process of seeing detailed pictures in your mind will assist you in your success. Your imagination is so very powerful, and by using visualization, you can retrain your subconscious mind to bring about the new experience you desire. Your brain doesn't know the difference between what you're thinking and what's in your current reality. Amazing things will start to happen when you begin to visualize. When you imagine pictures, the universe begins to arrange things in the background to make your visualization your reality. The right opportunities may show up at your doorstep, you might be guided to amazing solutions to your problems, and, after a little time, you can even see that the answers to "how" you will achieve reveal themselves right before your very eyes.

Some of the most talented athletes use visualization to help them break world records, win championships, and push themselves farther than ever thought humanly possible. Michael Jordan was a master at visualizing making that shot, doing that slam dunk, and winning that game. Record-setting Olympic medal winner, Michael Phelps, played the movie of "the perfect swim" each night before going to sleep, imagining winning each race. At a very young age, Tiger Woods' father taught the future golf champion about visualizing exactly where he wanted that ball to go. Olympic teams also use visualization. They even bring psychologists as part of their team to help them visualize their success. The athletes visualize themselves perfectly executing their craft. You might be thinking, "Okay, these are sport stars. They're gifted. How does this work for me?" The simple answer is that visualization works for you because it isn't just for athletes.

I began to visualize when I was an elementary school teacher. As I went to bed every night, I would think about the lessons that I had planned for the next day. I would go through my day, subject by subject, imagining myself teaching those lessons. I imagined myself standing in front of the classroom having the undivided attention of my students. I thought about my lessons being executed perfectly with all of the materials I needed to instruct the class. I also visualized that the children were well-behaved, engaged in the activities I guided, successful at completing their tasks, and excelling in their assessments. This helped send me off to dreamland with less worry and less stress about managing my classroom. Guess what happened when I woke up the next day and went off to school? I'd go through that day and it was just as I had imagined it the night before.

A bride begins to visualize her wedding day as soon as that ring is placed on her finger (maybe even sooner)! I know I did! Throughout the entire planning process, she focuses on images to create that perfect day. As she flips through bridal magazines, the images of her favorite items catch her eye, and she begins to focus more clearly on what she likes and what she doesn't like. While looking at floral arrangements, she can see and even smell the arrangement she'll hold as she walks down the aisle. As she gets fitted in her wedding gown, she closes her eyes and imagines being in her new husband's arms as they dance their first dance as husband and wife. While finalizing details at the reception hall, she samples the food and picks out the perfect cake. While falling asleep, she practices repeating her vows while gazing into the eyes of the love of her life. The bride-to-be smiles as she picks out the song list for the reception and sees herself dancing and singing along with her bridesmaids to their favorite song. This is how visualization and using images work to create that experience you desire.

SELECTING YOUR "CELEBRATORY MOMENT"

When I'm coaching a client who wants to achieve something really big, one of the first exercises we do is choose a Celebratory Moment. For a race car driver, the Celebratory Moment could be standing on the car, arms raised in victory as fireworks and confetti cannons erupt while the crowd roars with excitement. Your Celebratory Moment will actually transcend your goal. It's not just about that number you want to hit or that project you want to complete. It's the entire experience around the accomplishment that you want to create. You want to hit that lofty goal, but why? Why even bother? It's really about enjoying life and creating that next experience. Choosing your Celebratory Moment will become the focal point of your visualizations.

> **"I have been visualizing myself every night for the past four years standing on the podium having the gold placed around my neck."**
>
> ~ Megan Quann, Olympic gold medalist

If you're writing a book, it's not just about the book being written, but all of the other wonderful experiences surrounding it. Do you want the book completed because you want more public speaking engagements? Do you want to be invited to book signings where you meet your beloved readers and hear their praise? Do you want to be interviewed on podcasts, radio interviews, or television shows to spread your message and reach a larger audience? Are you writing the book to use as a resource for your workshop attendees or coaching clients?

If you have a revenue goal, it's really not just about the money. It's about the effect that more money will have on your business or your personal life. Will it mean more rest and relaxation while you vacation with your friends or family? Will the additional revenue mean being able to expand your team? Will experiencing more abundance help you move into that bigger office or buy your dream home?

If you're striving to achieve a prestigious award, what is driving you to do so? Is it the experience of you receiving it, just like it was for me in The Big Drive? Can you imagine yourself being announced as the winner, being handed the trophy and giving your acceptance speech, or being recognized as a leader in your field? Maybe your Celebratory Moment is you standing on the podium with a medal placed around your neck and reveling in your victorious moment.

It's important to begin reflecting on the moment of celebration when you've achieved your dreams or goals. Choose your Celebratory Moment to hold in your mind. Visualize and bring clearer images into your mind so the universe can start to work on your behalf and bring things into alignment to allow for your success.

One of my longtime clients, Lisa, asked me to coach her as she desired to become a finalist in Infusionsoft's Small Business ICON contest (formerly the Ultimate Marketer contest). I had her start visualizing that she was chosen as a finalist, that she was on the stage speaking in front of the audience. A few weeks later, she called to tell me she was selected as one of the three finalists! First, I congratulated her and nearly fell out of my chair with excitement. Then I said, "Okay Lisa, now it's time to change your visualization. It's not just you up on stage speaking. Now, it's them calling your name, announcing you as the winner." That became her Celebratory Moment, and she imagined that moment night after night as she prepared to present at the conference. Luckily, I was there, sitting in the front row, to witness the moment Lisa's name was announced as the Small Business ICON winner 2014. Her visualization had become her reality.

Another client of mine hired me as her visualization coach to help her and her team achieve their fourth quarter goals. During one of her coaching calls, I prompted her to choose her Celebratory Moment. I asked, "Is it having the CEO shake your hand, telling you, 'Job well done?' Is it gathering your team in a circle where you tell them the great news?" She knew immediately what it was going to be. It was her, her team, and their spouses having a wonderful celebration dinner during a staycation at a beautiful local resort. She began to visualize her Celebratory Moment and, in her mind, she practiced giving a toast to her amazing team at the dinner table. In a few short weeks, they had not only met their company goals, but had crushed them! She lived out her Celebratory Moment, by giving that speech to thank everyone for all their hard work.

Again, remember the importance of your Celebratory Moment is to transcend your goal. It gives you a purpose and something to look forward to experiencing. The Celebratory Moment answers the question, "Why am I even doing this?" It's time for you to select your Celebratory Moment, so you can begin to visualize how you're going to celebrate your victory. Here are some ideas that may inspire you to choose your Celebratory Moment:

- Gathering with your team, your friends, and/or your family for a victory party.
- Shaking the hand of your CEO and hearing the words, "Job well done!"
- Relaxing on the beach, listening to the ocean waves.
- Raising a glass and giving a toast to the people who helped make your goals a reality.
- Being announced as the winner and recipient of that prestigious award.

- Holding your new book in your hands.

- Looking at a banner that you get to display in your department or in your office showing the metrics you hit or exceeded.

- Holding a team huddle where you announce that together you crushed your goals and telling everyone how proud you are of the team.

- Seeing your name on the marquee for the debut of your Broadway musical.

- Having a housewarming party to gather your family together in celebration of your new dream home.

- Taking your entire team and their families on a trip to Disneyland to celebrate your achievement.

VISUALIZATION SECRETS

Once you have chosen your Celebratory Moment, you can start to visualize that experience in more detail. You are going to replay a moving picture in your mind repeatedly, adding more details each and every time. Learning to visualize takes practice. Build the skill, but have fun while doing it! When you practice visualization, you are going to let your mind open up and allow yourself the time to daydream. Show the universe exactly what you want by imagining your moment of achievement. You'll begin to attract new opportunities and keep yourself motivated as you move toward your goals.

> **"Visualize this thing you want. See it, feel it, believe in it. Make your mental blueprint and begin."**
>
> ~ Robert Collier

Over the years, I've been practicing and enhancing my visualization techniques. Here are some of my secrets for the most powerful visualizations:

1. **Create an ambience.** Taking the time to create the perfect atmosphere will allow you to concentrate and enjoy your visualization. Find a time when it's quiet so you won't be

disturbed or distracted. The last thing you want to hear is the neighbor's dog barking or your phone ringing unexpectedly to startle you from your relaxed state. To get you in the mood, you may even develop a ritual where you play some relaxing music, light a candle, or diffuse some essential oils. Finding a place where you can get comfortable is essential. You could try sitting in your favorite chair, heading outside into nature, or getting cozy in your bed. Sit back or lie down and settle in. Once you've set the mood and eliminated distractions, you simply close your eyes and imagine your Celebratory Moment.

2. **Imagine in pictures and words.** You'll want to imagine your Celebratory Moment in pictures and words. Just like in The Big Drive visualization that I shared with you, every night I imagined what that room looked like, seeing my friends and family in the audience, and exactly what I was going to wear that evening. I also practiced the words I'd say that night, especially during my acceptance speech. I said that speech so many times in my mind that I had it memorized by heart when I went up on stage to give it to the audience during the actual awards ceremony. When you visualize, it's like a moving picture. Imagine a movie playing in your mind. You're looking all around, living out the event, and thinking about the words that you're saying and hearing, too.

   - **The Place:** Look around you and imagine the location. What does it look like? Are you inside or outside?

   - **The Time:** Imagine the time of year, the time of day, and even the weather!

   - **The Events:** What is happening step-by-step? What is going on around you? What are you saying?

   Get super detailed about the images you envision. Remember, you're the director of the movie and the main actor at the same time. Imagine what that movie looks like in pictures to bring a clearer focus.

3. **Visualize in the first person.** When you visualize, you imagine the movie of your special moment playing in your mind. However, this is not the kind of movie where you're sitting

in the audience, eating popcorn, and looking up at the big screen, watching things happen from afar. No, instead YOU play the starring role of this movie so everything should come from your perspective. What you see around you should come from your own two eyes. When you look down, imagine exactly what you're wearing. Look directly at the other cast of characters and see their reactions from your perspective. A client once asked me, "Do I have to visualize this way? What if I don't?" If you don't visualize this way, you create a disconnect between you and your goals. It's essential to step into your movie and view everything from your perspective. Imagining from the first person is a more effective way for you to move toward your dreams.

4. **Imagine others celebrating with you.** Who will celebrate and enjoy your success with you? Remember you don't create alone, so think about others who can co-create this experience with you. Think about sharing your special day with your loved ones, your supporters, and other important people in your life. Imagine the people who want you to achieve your goal and want to enjoy your Celebratory Moment with you. Include them in your visualizations. They can be the members of your pit crew. They can be the people wanting to hire you for this new service you want to provide, to read the book you publish, to go with you on that vacation. Bring the images more into focus by seeing their faces and thinking about what they are saying to you. Identifying the people who want you to achieve your goals will give your visualization a bigger purpose and bring you a step closer to the checkered flag.

5. **Incorporate all of your senses.** When you visualize, it's also important to imagine your Celebratory Moment with all of your senses. As you picture the event, think about not only what you see, but what you experience with all of your senses.

   ▪ **What do you hear?** Is it the silverware clanking on the plates during the dinner, the audience clapping, or your name being called out as the winner?

- **What do you smell?** Is it the fresh ocean water, the food being served for dinner, or the sweet flowers in the table centerpiece?

- **What do you taste?** If you're eating, what does the food taste like? Can you imagine savoring each bite?

- **What do you feel?** Use your sense of touch to imagine how everything feels as you reach out to touch it. Think about the sand between your toes, the soft velvet covering the chair you're sitting on, or even the warmth of the spotlight shining on you.

When you incorporate all of your senses into your visualization, it brings more focus, more detail, and more clarity to it. You will become fully immersed into the experience you've been imagining.

6. **Experience the feelings of the moment.** While you visualize, allow yourself to experience the feelings or emotions of the moment. Think about how you'll feel while living out your Celebratory Moment and actually begin to experience those positive feelings while you're visualizing. When you think about the moment you pass by that checkered flag and have achieved your goal, you will have made a huge accomplishment. It's time to revel in your glory, or at least imagine it for now.

Maybe you will feel some of the following feelings or emotions:

- **Excitement** - Can you feel the butterflies of excitement?

- **Joy** - Are you going to cry tears of joy for reaching your goal?

- **Gratitude** - Can you feel the appreciation you have for this moment and for everyone who helped you along the way?

- **Pride** - Will a sense of pride emanate from you as you hold your head up high and enjoy the recognition?

- **Relaxation** - Can you imagine the stress releasing from your body as you relax during that vacation?

Allow the feelings to originate in your heart and rush through your body. Focusing on the feelings of the moment will trick your subconscious mind into believing it's already happened.

7. **Make it a daily habit.** Make it a habit by sitting down to visualize at the same time each day. Maybe it's during a work break or right after your morning walk. A really effective time to visualize is right after you meditate, when you've quieted your mind and gotten rid of the chatter. You can also try to visualize as you fall asleep. I've mentioned before that the things you're thinking right before you fall asleep stay with you through the night. Your subconscious mind holds those thoughts as you sleep.

When are the best times to visualize daily?

- Upon waking up
- During your shower
- During a break
- After you meditate
- During your morning or afternoon walk
- As you fall asleep at night

Set aside this time each day so you can drift away and daydream! When you commit to visualizing daily, the images of you achieving your goals will become deeply ingrained in your subconscious mind. You will also keep yourself motivated and maintain excitement to keep you moving forward.

8. **Add more details every time.** At first your visualizations might seem vague and unclear, but each time you play the movie in your mind you can add new details to your special moment. Don't be afraid to have fun and get creative! Rehearse exactly what you're going to say. Imagine what you're going to wear. Let your imagination run wild with orchestrating the perfect celebration for crossing that finish line. You'll find that your visualization will begin to cross over into your daily life. For example, while shopping you may

come across that perfect champagne glass to hold up as you toast to your victory. You can then add this new detail to your visualization! Tell the universe exactly how you want this moment to play out and get clearer and more specific each day.

GET INTO GEAR

- Realize the role visualization plays in achieving your goals.

- Your Celebratory Moment helps you focus on the experience that you want to create for yourself.

- Find a quiet, relaxing place where you won't be disturbed and visualize your Celebratory Moment daily.

- Imagine your Celebratory Moment in pictures and words, incorporate all of your senses, and add more details each time you visualize it.

ACCELERATE TOWARD YOUR SUCCESS

1. Choose your Celebratory Moment. How are you going to celebrate once you've achieved your goal? Think about where you'll be, what you'll be doing, and who will be celebrating with you.

2. Begin to visualize daily. Start with maybe 5-10 minutes, but don't overwhelm yourself. Get quiet and begin exercising these muscles, because it takes time to develop them. Make visualizing a daily habit, and, in time, you'll see how powerful it is. Opportunities will come your way and what you experience will become aligned with your thoughts and images.

ON THE ROAD REFLECTIONS

Describe your Celebratory Moment in your journal. Be detailed as you write about the moment you see yourself achieving your goals. Tell the story of that moving picture you imagine in the first person and in the present tense.

What are some of the feelings you experience as you visualize your Celebratory Moment? Let your imagination run wild as you look ahead to your victory.

**Amazing things will start to happen
when you begin to visualize.**

CHAPTER

CUSTOMIZE YOUR RIDE

"Play is the highest form of research."

~ Albert Einstein

Everything up until now has been in your mind and in your head: the thoughts you've been thinking, the words you've been saying, and the pictures you've been imagining. Now it's time to deliberately bring them into the physical world. Anchor your new beliefs as you surround yourself with visual representations of your goal achievement. Drivers plan ahead to make the race car a physical representation of themselves by displaying their interests and showing their personalities. To help them envision the win, they turbocharge their engines, decorate the car with flashy colors and sponsorship images, and even add their own special touches, such as a good luck charm, to the inside of the vehicle. Bringing the victory into their physical world with these symbols, emblems, and traditions will carry them through to the end of the race. Learn how you too, can customize the vehicle that will bring you to your success!

CAMAROS AT EVERY TURN

When I first began on this journey to win the Camaro, I knew it would be important to surround myself with symbols and tokens that represented the achievement of my goal. Right away, I wanted to engage my creativity along with my husband and children. I bought some poster board and markers, and I printed pictures of Camaros to represent my success. My goal was to sell 50 software subscriptions to win the contest in those three months so I thought about ways to monitor my progress. I took a poster board and drew a thermometer. I thought, "Let's just start at the bottom and each time I sell a subscription, I can keep track by coloring in a different section." The kids grabbed a ruler to help me draw lines to make 50 sections, each one symbolizing a sale. We numbered the sections from 1 to 50 and created a color key at the bottom so we could identify different types of companies I sold to: financial planners, attorneys, dentists, etc. I took a picture of a Camaro and the logo from The Big Drive advertisement, and we pasted those at the top so we could keep our eyes on the prize.

Then, I turned to the kids and asked, "This would be really great to sell all of these. If I do, I want to reward you as well! What prize would you each like to receive? Think big! Something you **really** want." I wanted them to have some ownership in this contest and a vested interest in our success, too. Our son chose the colossal Lego Death Star set. Being a big *Star Wars* fan and a Lego fanatic, the Death Star was always something he wished to have. Our two girls each selected their own iPad mini. We printed and pasted pictures of their grand prizes on the thermometer poster and tacked it up on the living room wall where we could all see it every day. Now we were working as a team and visualizing together. It brought a new sense of accountability to all of us.

I grabbed another poster board and created a vision board that was specifically focused on this contest. I added pictures of Camaros, a trophy, and other images that represented my victory. I added words and phrases to motivate and inspire me as I worked in my home office where I displayed this poster. While creating this board, I was bringing the images I had imagined during my visualizations out of my mind and into my physical world. I felt more focused and my belief was stronger than ever.

My husband came home one day and handed me a gift. He found a large 3-ring binder at the store with a Camaro on the front! He said, "Here's a binder for you to use. You can put your client notes in there and keep track of your prospects." What a wonderful surprise! I began to use it right away and placed it on my desk where I could look at it every day. I surrounded myself with Camaros, wonderful reminders and motivators of what I was working toward.

As a family, we started noticing other Camaros driving on the street. One weekend we took a little drive up to Sedona, which is just a couple hours north of where we live. As we headed out on our family adventure, Joe had the idea to play a little game and invited us to have some fun. He suggested, "Let's count how many Camaros we see along the way." Throughout this game, we noticed the variety of options out there: the different wheels, spoilers, and colors. Some had racing stripes, and we even saw some really cool classics driving around, too. That day we counted more than 50 Camaros during our round trip! It seemed like at every turn, there was a Camaro. We even spotted a yellow Camaro in our neighborhood with long black eyelashes attached to the headlights. I swear that car was batting her eyelashes at me saying, "Can't wait to see your new car, Honey!" It was a great way for us to focus our attention and attract a new Camaro easily into our lives.

To further my focus on my intention, I worked on another project. I found a shoe box and covered it with blank paper so that I could decorate it with representations of my goal achievement. I made a pit stop at Michael's, a craft store, to buy stickers and other adornments to decorate my box. As I took out all of the supplies, our daughter, Jillian, came and sat with me, very curious about what I was doing. I talked to her about my goal and how this box would help me create it. Eagerly, she helped me put stickers of race cars, trophies, and award ribbons on the outside of the box. For the inside of the box, I cut strips of paper, and I wrote "I am" statements on them: I am an inspiration to others, I am a winner, and I am a success. As I placed the strips of paper inside the box, I read them aloud one by one. I closed the box and placed it on my dresser where I could see it every day.

One day when the kids were at school, my husband and I decided to play hooky and headed to a Chevy dealership for an even closer look at Camaros by getting in them and driving them. What a rush to look at an entire row of Camaros in the lot! I enjoyed seeing the different upgrades, sat inside of them, and even got to take one for a test drive. I loved the new car smell, put my hands on the steering wheel and imagined it was mine as I drove it on the nearby streets. Engaging my creativity in all of these ways and surrounding myself with this car turbocharged my motivation. It made me feel as if my success was in the here and now.

STIMULATE YOUR CREATIVE ENERGY

You can engage your creativity by surrounding yourself with symbols of your goal achievement. Remember that you create with your thoughts, your images, and your actions. In previous chapters, you've worked on thinking positively about your goal, saying positive words, and visualizing images in your mind, so now it's time to take some action.

Albert Einstein, one of the most brilliant minds of the modern age, was asked how he discovered the theory of relativity. His response was, "I wasn't looking for it. It just dropped in while I was listening to my favorite piece of music." One of his biggest regrets, too, is that he didn't play more often. When he played, he realized he experienced his highest levels of creativity and greatest success. I invite you to take some time for play to allow those ideas to drop in, like Einstein did.

As you take some time to play and create the projects outlined in this chapter, you will stimulate your creative energy, customize your ride, and turbocharge your engine. When I pass out the glue sticks, markers, puffy paints, and glitter during a creative workshop with a leadership team, some of the attendees are really skeptical and doubtful, wondering how engaging in this type of activity will be beneficial to their success. Some have even felt a bit uncomfortable during the process. However, when the class is complete and they have a decorated box, board, or poster in hand, they leave with a stronger sense of confidence, a renewed hope, and bright ideas about how to achieve their goals. I've witnessed stressed out, anxious groups of attendees transform as their stress is alleviated, and they walk out smiling. The final product gets displayed in their work area and serves as a reminder of the good to come.

You might be thinking, "How can this be? What good could possibly come from arts and crafts when I have so much work to get done?" Here are some of the benefits of getting your craft on:

- **Gain a clearer focus.** By finding symbols of your goal achievement and creating projects, you're going to fine-tune your focus about exactly what you want to bring into your life. You're going to use your imagination even more than you've done before and focus more clearly on your goal achievement and what your Celebratory Moment will look like. As you draw and select pictures, you will make choices about what you do want and what you don't want. Your preferences will become more and more apparent. For me, I began to ask myself, "Which color do I prefer, the silver, black, or red Camaro? Would I like a spoiler, racing stripes, or silver or black wheels?" We create with focus, and these activities will help you pay attention to the details and see your success more clearly.

- **Boost your confidence.** As you participate in these creative activities, you will gain the support of your subconscious mind while increasing your confidence levels. While you're engaging your creativity, you're going to have fun and think positively throughout the activity. As you repeat positive affirmations and enjoy thinking about the end result, you will become more confident and realize the possibility is closer than you first imagined. You will see your goal as already attained and maintain your state of belief.

- **Get unstuck.** When you take a break in your logical, analytical, and linear patterns, you can open you mind to new possibilities. Taking time to play by creating a poster board, picture collage, or arrangement of objects, will help you make a shift in your habits and allow for bright ideas to drop in like they did for Einstein. Get out of your own way by taking time to play and be creative. You'll allow for new opportunities and ideas to enter your life, bringing you leaps and bounds closer to your goals.

- **Show commitment.** As you begin to search for pictures, stickers, and tokens that represent your goal achievement and display them around you, you are making a firm commitment. This process is going to invite your goal into your world. It's like you are turning on the porch light welcoming the goal to enter your life by saying, "Okay, I'm here and I'm ready! I am serious about this." The result is that you will anchor your new beliefs. Your determination will become more solid and unwavering as you get clearer in your focus and begin to be more creative.

It's time to customize your ride for the journey ahead. Let your guard down, be open, and allow your creativity to flow! So, get out your glue gun, break open the craft bin, and get ready to play!

SURROUND YOURSELF WITH TOKENS OF YOUR GOAL ACHIEVEMENT

During the Big Drive, I surrounded myself with many tokens and reminders of being the grand prize winner of the Camaro. I kept my client notes in a 3-ring binder with a picture of a Camaro on the front. I had pictures surrounding me in my workspace. It seemed like Camaros were coming out of the woodwork. Everywhere I looked, there they were! As you work toward your goals, start thinking about ways you can have constant reminders around you and keep your eyes open for fun tokens, knick knacks, and pictures. It will almost be uncanny how often these pop up around you. You can buy some that you find at the store, take screenshots of the images you see on the computer, or just acknowledge them with a smile and a nod when they cross your path.

Michele, a member of one of my group coaching programs called "The Mompreneur Mindset" is an essential oils distributor in a network marketing company. She had set a goal to earn a promotion to the silver level in the organization. To accomplish that, she needed to consistently sell a certain amount each month while also recruiting new members to her team. I recommended she begin to think "silver" and to bring silver into her everyday life. We discussed her wearing silver jewelry, placing silver items on her dresser, and even writing in silver when she could! During our next call, she shared with the group how she had begun to surround herself with silver and had even gotten a pedicure, getting silver polish on her toes. I was so pleased to hear that! Silver became the norm for her. Everywhere she looked, she saw the flashy color to remind her of her desire to be promoted. Within no time, she achieved the silver level, and we celebrated her victory. When it became time for the next level, the gold level, I said, "Okay, you're going to switch it up now and begin to surround yourself with **gold** instead." I'll bet she can't wait for the diamond level!

I love to send my private coaching clients letters, notes, and gifts that I call, "Pick-me-ups." I send them mementos, tokens, pictures, and wall hangings with their mantra or other reminders of their goals. While I was working with one of my clients, her team's mantra was "Believe 2014!" It was the holiday season, and as I was doing my shopping, I came across a beautiful angel ornament with "Believe" engraved on her skirt and she was holding a star with the year "2014." The entire team received the ornament and placed them on trees in their department, on their desks, or brought them home to display. It was a token they could all look at and remember how important it was to believe in themselves. Now, the angel ornaments serve as reminders of their great accomplishments that year.

I visited one of my corporate clients to walk the floor, check in on team morale, and offer an encouraging word as they neared a fast-approaching deadline. The department's Celebratory Moment was to take a day trip as an entire team to Disneyland. When I arrived, I was so pleased to see how they had surrounded themselves with representations of their goal achievement. In fact, the whole floor looked a lot like the "Happiest Place on Earth!" Mickey Mouse cutouts adorned their desks and cubicles. Pathways in their workspace had wooden sign posts directing staff to Thunder Mountain or to the nearest churros. They had immersed themselves in all things Disneyland to motivate and inspire them in their daily work.

I asked one of the leaders how decorating the workspace this way impacted the thoughts, mindset, and actions of the entire staff. He said, "These served as constant messaging to remove doubt. It was a hard goal we had set, and we were understaffed. Decorating this way elevated the morale of our entire team to get us back to belief."

You can see how this can be a beneficial exercise to bring reminders of your Celebratory Moment into your physical world. Surrounding yourself with tokens can be fun! Don't forget to involve others in your creations to work as a team and to help keep you all positive and upbeat toward your goals.

Here are some items to search for, projects to create, or actions to take to get you started on customizing your ride:

- Make a picture collage using images that represent your goal achievement.

- Add a computer screensaver with your mantra, an image representing your big win, or a picture of your dream vacation spot.

- Find "parking spots" in a room, on a shelf, or on your desk to display tokens that represent your accomplishments.

- Be specific with the tokens you place around you. For instance, if you're dreaming of a trip to Hawaii, find a dancing hula girl toy to put on your dashboard, nightstand, or desk.

- Superimpose your name on an image or object. For example, you can glue your name to a trophy base, add your photo to the executive team bios page, or design a book cover with your name listed as the author. You can use free, graphic design programs like Pixlr.com or PicMonkey. com to create your designs.

- Take a test drive in your dream car.

- Visit the location that's part of your Celebratory Moment. Drive through the neighborhood where you'd love to live, visit the restaurant where you'll host your celebratory dinner, or buy a book that tells you about the popular sites in the city you've always wanted to see.

CREATE A FOCUS BOARD

Shortly after we returned home from a family cruise to the Mexican Riviera, my husband came home from work one day and said, "Janette, I have to tell you the craziest thing! I just realized that every time I went to the restaurant near my office for lunch, I looked at a poster of a cruise ship that was on the window of a travel agency across the way. Today was the first day I realized that this was the same exact cruise ship that we just went on! Not just any cruise ship, the same exact one!" We were amazed how the simple act of glancing at that picture every day brought that experience into his life. Now, he also had the desire to take his family on a cruise and took actions toward planning and saving for it. A few years later, we taped a picture of a cruise to Italy on our bathroom mirror and got to enjoy that trip. Traveling to Australia is on my bucket list so the next picture I'll display will be the Sydney Opera House!

A simple poster with a few words can be a great Focus Board, but you can get even more detailed as well. Our son, Joey, is a master at creating these. As a youngster completely obsessed with Legos, he'd keep tabs on the newest line of Lego sets by checking online. He knew when the next set was going to be released. He created posters and lists with the name, set number, and price for each. He'd clear a space on a shelf or in a drawer and tape the poster up above it. He had such clear focus about what he wanted and instinctively created a Focus Board to help him bring it into his physical world. My husband and I would eagerly wait to see how these sets would come to him. Sometimes he'd save his own money, and we'd order them online. Sometimes he'd receive them as birthday presents. One of our favorite memories was when his grandparents surprised him for Christmas with a discontinued set he wished for. They found it online and had it shipped all the way from England!

Some of the frustrations that I've heard from people is they get all excited about setting goals at the beginning of the new year and maybe even make a vision board. However, by the end of the year they look at the board and think, "I didn't really accomplish much, and I'm really frustrated. I just don't know which direction to go." The problem that I often uncover is that they lacked clarity before beginning a project like a vision board.

Vision boards are great for dreaming, but a **Focus Board** can help you achieve your goals faster. While working with clients during a VIP Day or workshop, I guide them in creating a board specifically about one particular goal, and we're very intentional about what goes on that board. If you've been following the processes outlined in this book, you're clear on what you want, you believe you can achieve your goals, and you have started to think positively. You have also selected and started visualizing your Celebratory Moment. Now is the perfect time for you to engage in a project that will help you focus.

Are you getting excited about making your own Focus Board? I hope you are! Here are the steps for getting it done:

1. **Brainstorm a list of ideas.** Grab your journal or a sheet of paper and take some time to brainstorm ideas, words, and phrases that relate to your goal achievement.

2. **Gather materials.** Find a poster board, cork board, or large sheet of paper for displaying your items. Gather up some art supplies: pens, markers, scissors, glue, and stickers of letters, numbers, and symbols. Don't be shy about grabbing some glitter pens and other fancy embellishments to make things fun! Then, begin to collect pictures of your goal achievement by cutting out images from magazines or printing some from the Internet.

3. **Make your Focus Board.** Block off uninterrupted time to work on your project. Set up your workspace and begin to place the items on your poster board. I like to lay out the pictures first. Then, I place the words in the empty spaces and near the appropriate pictures. When everything looks good, go ahead and glue everything down. Finally, add the stickers, sparkles, and other embellishments for the finishing touch. There is no wrong way. Let your creativity run wild!

4. **Enjoy the process.** This shouldn't be a chore. Have a good time! Have your theme song playing in the background, enjoy a refreshing beverage of your choice, and maybe pop a bowl of popcorn to snack on while you work. Consider inviting a friend, your spouse, your children, or members of your team to do this with you. When you're working on this with somebody else you can encourage and support each other, share ideas, and have a blast at the same time!

5. **Display it.** Now that your Focus Board is finished, it's time to proudly display your work of art! Put it somewhere prominent where you can see it and look at it daily. It might be in your office, in your bedroom, or maybe on the back of the closet door so when you get dressed every day you're able to look at it and really focus. As you look at it, repeat your positive affirmations or imagine your Celebratory Moment.

Allow your inner child to come out and play. The benefits are magnificent! You'll fine-tune your focus, gain the support of your subconscious mind, and think positively about your goals. Also, you will have given a formal invitation for the goals to enter your life.

ASSEMBLE AN ACHIEVE BOX

My coach, Sonia, introduced me to the idea of creating what she calls an alchemy box to help me achieve my heart's desires. She described how I could take a box, decorate it on the outside, and place items on the inside. The word, alchemy, means to make a transformation. I learned that when you engage in creating this box, you transform your thoughts and images and bring them into your physical world.

This idea was really intriguing to me so I began to create these boxes. Once or twice a year, I would decorate the outside with symbols and pictures of my hopes and dreams while placing paper strips containing my affirmations and little tokens on the inside. The act of making an intention and sending it off into the universe sped up the progress of my goal achievement. At first, I decorated the box with all sorts of ideas and aspirations. Then, I added a little twist and got even more focused - one goal for each box. My results were amplified.

As I started having my clients make these "Achieve Boxes," the impact not only helped them accomplish their goals, but I've proudly witnessed a ripple effect of groups of people coming together to make their boxes, too. The word started to spread. Soon, many others reached out telling me about their desire to create their own boxes! I love to see my own children making this a regular practice in their daily lives to use the tools and strategies I teach my clients. It's second nature for them to narrow in on what they'd like to achieve, raid my craft bins, and emerge from my home office with Focus Boards and Achieve Boxes in hand.

Jianna, our 11-year old daughter, told me all about her desire to write and publish her own book, a story about two friends. She knew exactly what was next for her: to bring those thoughts and images into her physical world by getting crafty. Her beautiful Achieve Box is adorned with phrases and pictures and now sits on her nightstand to serve as reminder of her intention. I'm her biggest fan and her crew chief, and I can't wait to watch her live out her Celebratory Moment at her very own book signing.

During a visit at a corporate client's office, I ran into my friend and client, Thomas. We talked about setting and achieving goals, and he told me how he saw a group of people making their Achieve Boxes in the office. He also confided in me, saying he secretly wanted to make one, too. I took that as a great opportunity to help so I got to work. I assembled the very first Achieve Box Kit and mailed it to him with a special note and directions inside.

Thomas wasn't much of a dreamer. He admits that he's perfectly happy playing it safe, making his lists, and checking things off his "to do" list. But, he gave it try! When it was done, he realized the power in making a declaration, writing it down, and making something that represented his goals. When I asked him how making this box impacted his mindset, he said, "It becomes a representation of my dreams. I cut out pictures and glue them to the box. I put on stickers and draw symbols. I write phrases. I really concentrate and focus while decorating the box with numbers, words, and pictures that represent my goals." Now, Thomas makes it a quarterly habit to set goals and make a new Achieve Box. As he creates his box, he asks himself, "Is this what I really, really want?" This process allows him to dream more often, narrow in on his goals, and make a plan to get it done.

An Achieve Box can also be a great team-building exercise. My client, Geoff, participated in a creative workshop I facilitated for a leadership team. The objectives of the day were to get everyone to achieve a state of belief regarding their department goals. Each member of the team created an Achieve Box that day and proceeded to take massive action, and with new, innovative ideas and drive, they were able to crush their goals that quarter.

After some time had passed, Geoff and I had a conversation about that workshop. He reflected on the Achieve Box he made, telling me, "It wasn't just the box; it was getting together as a team. The activity was very powerful." It was something different and a time for the leadership team to come together, have fun, and make a commitment to our goals. Geoff added, "During that activity, we declared what was going to happen that quarter and put them in the box. As we walked out of the door with our boxes in hand, that was the starting point for all of us."

Here are directions to get started on your Achieve Box:

1. **Find your box.** For this project you'll need a box with blank, undecorated sides. You can go to a craft or office supply

store to purchase a small box. You could also dig through your closet and find a shoe box to use for the project. If it already has some printing on the side, just cover it with blank paper.

2. **Gather materials.** Round up the art supplies like pens, markers, scissors, and glue, just like you did in the Focus Board activity. Find some stickers that have letters, numbers, phrases, and pictures that go with your goal achievement. Finally, you'll need blank strips of paper that will fit inside of your box.

3. **Decorate your box.** The next step is to find a workspace and start decorating the sides of the box. Glue the pictures on the sides, grab a marker and start writing your wishes, and place some stickers, too. Stay as focused as possible. Try to create your box with only one to three goals in mind. Even better yet, make one box per goal! Don't forget to have fun and allow yourself to express your creativity.

4. **Write statements.** Once the box has been decorated, incorporate some positive affirmations into this activity. On your strips of paper, write your "I Believe" and "I Am" statements, and place them inside the box. I suggest writing 8-10 statements. Then, one by one, read each aloud as you place it in the box. Put the lid on the box and say, "So be it," to seal in your intentions!

5. **Display the box.** Place the box where you can see it every day, on your dresser, on your desk, etc. When I work with executives, I have them place it on their desk or in their main meeting area, somewhere where they can look at it and see it every day. If you are super proud of your box, which most people usually are, share a picture of your creation on social media using the hashtag #AchieveBox. That will help spread the word and share the fun of the project.

I've been making Achieve Boxes for a few years now, and I have a wonderful collection of them now that I keep on my bedroom dresser. Once in a while, I open them up, look at the papers inside, and revel at all that I've accomplished throughout the years. It's become a family affair and a highly sought after workshop activity for my clients. Why not? Who doesn't need some time to play?

Begin to take the thoughts and images you've been thinking about and bring them into the physical plane. Engage your creativity and surround yourself with symbols of your sweet victory. Some of you may be thinking, "I don't think so! There's no way I'm going to get crafty!" My advice is to get over yourself and get busy customizing your beautiful ride (or Focus Board or box). How do you want your success to be and what do you want it to look like? The good news is that you can customize this win anyway you'd like! Only the sky (or a grumpy attitude) will limit you.

 ## GET INTO GEAR

- Be more observant of your surroundings to see cues that remind you of your goals.

- Transform your thoughts and images by bringing them into the physical world.

- Think positively and gain support from your subconscious mind.

- Surround yourself with reminders of your goal achievement, by printing a photo, choosing a token, or taking a test drive.

- Brainstorm ideas, gather materials, make a Focus Board, and place it in a prominent location so you can see it every day.

- Assemble and take a picture of your #AchieveBox and share it on social media.

- Anchor your new beliefs and allow for new ideas and new opportunities to enter your life.

 ## ACCELERATE TOWARD YOUR SUCCESS

1. Begin to find and display tokens of your goal achievement. Be on high alert for items that remind you of your goals and buy them or make them. The point is to surround yourself with these tokens one at a time, little by little.

2. Choose one of the following activities: either make a Focus Board or an Achieve Box. Go through this

process, enjoy it, engage your creativity, and watch the opportunities and the ideas drop in just like they did for Albert Einstein.

ON THE ROAD REFLECTIONS

Reinforce your intentions by writing your goals, the ones you jotted down on the slips of paper and placed in your Achieve Box and in your journal. Or, glue photos in your journal that represent your goals. Each night, you can look at them before you fall asleep so these positive images and words will remain with you throughout the night. Remember what you think about, you bring about. It's time to transform your thoughts and images and welcome them into your physical world.

**Invite your goal into your physical world to show
you are serious and committed to achieving it.**

PUT THE PEDAL TO THE METAL

"The difference between who we are and who we want to be is what we do."

~ Author Unknown

At this point in the journey, you are super focused, have the support you need, and are attracting new opportunities into your life. You're actually starting to feel the success. You're feeling belief and excitement because the ball is in motion, and you're gaining momentum. Now, it's time for you to take action. Action is one of the key ingredients to your victory, and you're going to find out how taking the right kind of action will accelerate your success. I'm going to share specific types of activities that you need to make a priority and give you some tips for getting it all done. We all have hectic lives so how can you fit this goal into your already busy schedule? Success is a combination of hard work, commitment, and dedication. It's time to hit the gas and get to work!

WHERE THE RUBBER MEETS THE ROAD

Whenever I talk about winning The Big Drive competition, I try to use phrases like "I **earned** the car in a sales competition." It wasn't just luck! No, my name wasn't pulled out of a hat. No, that car didn't just show up in my driveway one day. It wasn't that easy. I spent lots of time on personal development. I made a concerted effort at thinking positively, getting into new habits, and growing exponentially. At the same time, I took massive action and made sacrifices. In other words, I worked my tail off. I worked harder than I had ever worked before in my entire life.

After the competition started in late May, potential partners, leaders of large organizations, began to approach me. They wanted me to create systems for their members, to share what I had done in Infusionsoft for my own businesses and apply my marketing success secrets to their businesses. This presented me with a great opportunity: to sell subscriptions in large quantities to their members. These calls were coming seemingly out of nowhere, from sources I had never even expected. They were messages from the universe and guidance I was open to following. I needed to develop marketing campaigns for these vertical niches. I put all of my knowledge from marketing for our own businesses, and from my experience with my consulting clients, into systems for financial planners and estate planning attorneys. There was no manual for me to follow and no template for this process. I had to create it from scratch. It seemed quite daunting, but I was up for the challenge! I was prepared to do whatever it took to be the first one crossing the finish line.

The contest period ran from Memorial Day weekend until Labor Day weekend. It was summer time. The kids were home from school, and it would have been easy to sleep in and spend a big chunk of my days splashing around in the pool with them. Instead, I was getting up early in the morning before anybody else did, creating systems and processes that were scalable. It took me probably 10 times as long doing it this way, but I knew that I had to make this a process that could be duplicated by my team—the team that I had assembled to support me.

As I look back, I realize that it really took massive amounts of courage for me to take on so many clients at one time. I also knew deep down that I had everything I needed to be successful: my prior experience, my Infusionsoft skills, and my amazing team to support me.

During the competition, I trained virtual assistants who were local moms looking to work from home. I conducted live virtual software training sessions so they could learn how to configure and use Infusionsoft. I showed them how to replicate my system step-by-step and piece-by-piece. My instructions were extremely detailed so they could work independently. This would free me up to keep selling more and more. I also hired coaches to train new customers to use the software system. I showed them each campaign that I had designed, how each one was used, and how they could effectively explain the benefits and uses to these new customers I acquired. These coaches spent on average, 10 hours working with each new customer. I knew I only had so many hours in the day, so I relied on my team to help me. They were indispensable!

The next step was to provide ongoing service to customers and to continue testing all of the campaigns so we could revise and enhance the product. I conducted live group training sessions weekly for the customers and hosted question and answer calls, providing them with supporting documents and resources that would help them be successful. We took tons of action daily and engaged in activities that kept us moving forward. There were days that flew by from the heightened activity, and it was amazing how productive we could be! I found myself waking up in the middle of the night, energized with this new passion and profound excitement for not only the prize, but for all that I was accomplishing. There was a self-transformation occurring, all while I was helping others along the way.

I remember having a really keen sense of awareness to every opportunity, every prospect, and every idea that dropped in. I said, "Yes" more often and had more gumption to go ahead and give new things a try. As a result, I discovered I had a super strength, sales skills I never knew I had. I was "wheeling and dealing," explaining the benefits of my programs and helping prospects make a commitment with a confidence in me I never knew existed.

There was a lot of work to do to prepare for the arrival of this new car. I acted "as if" the car was already mine. We sold our minivan. I researched car insurance premiums. We made room for the new car in our garage. I knew getting organized was going to be key for managing the increased workload and to get it all done. I didn't have time to procrastinate. I figured if you snooze, you lose. I only had three months to sell more than I had sold in my entire career. And on top of that, I had stiff competition. The best sales producers in the industry were breathing down my neck every single day. I watched that leaderboard and kept track of my competitors so I could stay on top. Through hard work, commitment, dedication, and sacrifice, I inched closer and closer to the finish line!

TAKE MASSIVE ACTION

"Good things come to people who wait, but better things come to those who go out and get them."

~Anonymous

Remember that you create with your thoughts, your images, and your actions. The key word now is action. During this chapter, you will focus on action, because you don't create without it. You need to take productive, effective, and practical action. You can't just sit on your back porch or patio hoping and wishing your goals will just drop out of the sky. The difference between who you are and who you want to be is what you do, the action that you take. If you've chosen the right goals, taking action will be a no-brainer for you. Put the pedal to the metal, get your motivation into overdrive, and head as fast as you can toward that finish line! Going on a rampage of taking massive action isn't for the faint of heart! You must be up for the challenge and willing to embody the following:

- **Hard work -** You have to put in the work by completing the tasks that will bring about your goals. "Hard work" doesn't have to mean it has to be a chore. These tasks should be energizing and fulfilling because you know the end result, the realization of a dream: YOUR dream. Putting forth the time and energy will bring you the results you desire.

- **Commitment -** When you initially selected and wrote down your goals, you made a declaration. The next level is to keep your commitment, the promise you made to yourself, to seeing them through. You can show commitment through time, effort, and actions that support the achievement of your goals.

- **Dedication -** One of the questions you asked yourself while choosing your goals was, "Can I and will I show up to these goals every day?" These goals are important to you, so you must give them your loyalty, completely and wholeheartedly. Remain faithful and dedicated to the promise you made yourself and give it the constant support it deserves.

At this point, procrastination will be one of your worst enemies. Do not procrastinate! Do not think, "Well, I'll just work on that next week. That, I can do next month." No, there's no time for that. It's time for you to get to work. If you have, in fact, selected the right goals, the desire to work toward them will be strong. You may even be so energized that you find yourself waking up in the middle of the night and feeling the urge to get right out of bed and take action.

As you hit the gas and with your goals constantly on your mind, feel and enjoy the rush of excitement and a renewed passion for life. Jump in with both feet and don't look back! Those who take inspired action and follow opportunities are the winners in life. Successful people are more inclined to act than continue to prepare and only talk about achieving their goals. When an opportunity presents itself, take it!

Imagine you're in a race, the race toward your goals. It doesn't matter how you're going to get there. Whether it's by car, by horse, or by your own two feet, go ahead and start driving, galloping, or running as fast as you can, without looking back. As you take massive action, you will accelerate toward this finish line. You must consistently and continuously take action, the right kind of action, to keep your lead and stay ahead in this race to the checkered flag.

GET ORGANIZED

To help maximize your efforts, take some time to prepare, get organized, and make a simple plan. Just as you wouldn't go on a vacation without making the proper preparations, you need to be ready for your journey to success!

1. **Make a "to-do" list.** In his book, *Eat That Frog*, Brian Tracy indicates that people who work from a list increase their productivity by 25% or more! You've done your due diligence and should know what it will take to get there. Take out a

sheet of paper and start brainstorming a list of things you need to do in order to achieve your goals.

If your goal, your heart's desire, is that you want to take a vacation, here's a quick list to get you started:

- Set the dates
- Request vacation days at work
- Research hotels
- Book airline tickets
- Go shopping
- Arrange a pet-sitter
- Pack!

This will be your master list, and it will give you a clear path to follow. Consider the items on your list to be signposts or checkpoints along the journey. A "to-do" list breaks things down into smaller steps for you and can be an excellent tool for overcoming procrastination. You'll always have a reference point for what needs to get done during the time you've set aside to work on your goals. Plus, think of the sense of accomplishment you'll feel as you work through and check things off as you go! So, make your list, keep it handy, and refer to it daily.

2. **Prioritize your action items.** My grandfather taught me an acronym to help me prioritize: E.V.I.S.U. He lived by this concept whether it came to making a purchase decision to managing his "to-do" list. The letters of this acronym can help you classify and prioritize everything on your list, too:

E – Extremely important
V – Very important
I – Important
S – Somewhat important
U – Unimportant

When looking through your list of action items, you can ask yourself how important each one is to complete. Our

grandpa never went to bed until all the "extremely important" tasks on his list were done!

Remember the saying, "Many hands make light work."
While you are taking massive action, focus on the tasks
that you're good at, your unique abilities, and, when you
can, give others away to someone more capable. Glance
through the list again looking for tasks you can delegate to
the members of your pit crew. Next to the task, write the
name of the person who can help you.

What are the most important tasks you need to complete
in order to move closer to your goals? What needs to get
done now? What should you do first? Give each task a
due date to create a sense of urgency and to plan ahead.
Consider eliminating the items that are unimportant. Circle
a few tasks with an earlier due date, and you've got yourself
a great starting point.

3. **Gather resources.** Gather organizational resources to
dedicate to the completion of your goals. The better
organized you are, the more likely you will be able to
concentrate and follow through with your task list.

What materials do you need to get organized? Here are
some items to purchase:

- Binders and folders to keep important documents in
one place

- Whiteboard, poster board, or cork board for
brainstorming ideas and keeping track of metrics

- Bins, crates, and boxes to help you stay organized

- A pocket planner or calendar so you can keep on
top of your "to-do" list and manage your daily life

- A software program or app for managing your
workflow

Carve out some time to take a trip to Walmart, The Container
Store, or an office supply store and stock up on new tools and
supplies that will help you stay organized and keep you on
track. Make your workspace inviting by choosing colors and
designs that make you feel good. Have fun while picking out

color-coded labels and stackable drawers. Heck, maybe even pick up a handy label maker and get labeling! If you need help, ask! Find a friend who has a love for all things organization, collects sticky note pads and fancy paper clips, and has an affinity for finding ideas on Pinterest. You might even hire an organizational consultant who can help you clear out the clutter and create new systems. You'll feel energized and will be ready to tackle those "to-do's" every day!

4. **Create a schedule.** Make time in your calendar and daily routine to dedicate to your goals. If your desire is to get fit, how often will you commit to exercising? When will you prepare healthy meals and snacks? Develop a yearly, monthly, weekly, and daily schedule. Block off the time in your schedule and do whatever it takes to stick to it. If you're working on a project, such as writing a blog or finishing up a new website, can you block off just 15 minutes a day to keep you moving toward that goal? If you've selected a date for that vacation that you're planning, get it in your calendar and arrange everything else around it.

During the time you've set aside, commit to doing the activities that will bring about your goals. Create boundaries and communicate them to your family, co-workers, and/or customers. Eliminate distractions so you can focus. Getting organized by writing your "to-do" list, prioritizing your action items, gathering the right resources, and creating a schedule and seeing it through will demonstrate your commitment and dedication to your goals.

WORK TOWARD YOUR GOAL

> **"The big secret in life is that there is no secret.**
> **Whatever your goal,**
> **you can get there if you are willing to work."**
>
> ~ Oprah Winfrey

Unfortunately, your success will not magically fall into your lap. You've got to work for it, sometimes putting forth effort like you've never given before in your entire life. I invite you to show up and stay committed to your goals every day by working toward them one step at a time. You have control over your thoughts, images, and actions, so you can get there! You also have your list of "to-do's" and the time blocked off to get it done so put your nose to the grindstone and get to work. As you take massive action, you are going to gain momentum and see things unfold right before your very eyes.

Hit the gas and accelerate towards the finish line by doing the following:

1. **Take small steps.** Start your day by glancing at your "to-do" list and asking yourself, "Who do I need to reach out to today to complete something on my list?" Can you email or call somebody to get the answers you need or to delegate a task? That's the first order of business. Once you've finished, punch through your list. Cross things off, one item at a time, as you complete them. It's rewarding when you can start seeing things get checked off; it shows that you're accomplishing something.

2. **Set a time frame.** In her book, *Get It Done*, my friend and colleague Sam Bennett, writes about going from procrastination to creative genius in 15 minutes a day. That's all it takes to get things done, 15 minutes! She actually calls it your "Fifteen Minutes of Fame" and recommends setting a timer for yourself. This is the time that you're showing up and taking action towards your projects and goals. And, don't let anything else distract you during that time: no Facebook, no cell phone, no emails, no daydreaming. When you focus, you'll be amazed at how much you can get done! You may even be inspired to go longer than the 15 minutes. If so, then go with it!

3. **Reward yourself.** Think about ways to motivate yourself to get your work completed. What will it take to get it done? Maybe it's a little reward for a job well done such as some time for playing Candy Crush, browsing around on Facebook, or enjoying a Caramel Macchiato from Starbucks.

I attended a writer's retreat last year in Sedona, Arizona, hosted by the amazing duo, Betsy Rapoport and Pamela

Slim. In regards to helping us write, they recommended setting a timeframe for focused work, too. They encouraged us, "Just take 15 minutes, half an hour, or whatever you think you can commit to and dedicate it to your writing. And then, after that time period, when your timer goes off, reward yourself." They invited us to think of simple and immediate ways to reward our focused activity. You could recognize your efforts and spoil yourself by drinking a cocktail by the pool, reading in bed with a bowl of homemade popcorn, or playing with your kids.

When hitting bigger milestones throughout your journey, reward yourself for taking action and give yourself a bonus for staying committed. How about a shopping trip, a day at a health spa, a hike in the mountains, or a date night with your significant other? Keep refueling as needed along the road!

4. **Use your time wisely.** My client, Mike Staver, a leadership coach, and best-selling author, trains leaders around the world to engage in "High Gain Activity" in order to get maximum results. He warns against being someone who insists on doing everything and who has trouble letting go of control to others. Mediocre results and slow progress can be the result of not using your time wisely. Mike poses the question, "What are the two activities that when you do them have the most productive impact on your business or goals?" By focusing on these productive activities, the work you excel at, you will have big-time success.

My husband and I teach our staff to engage in productive activity also. We classify tasks throughout the day as green light, yellow light, and red light activities. Here are descriptions of each:

- **Green light** - Activities that move you toward your goals. They are productive, time bound, and revenue generating.

- **Yellow light** - Routine tasks that are necessary and need your attention, but are less pressing.

- **Red light -** Activities that keep your from your goals. Time wasters, bad habits, and mindless behaviors must be off limits during your action sessions!

To help me manage my time and be more efficient, I practice "Creative Multi-tasking" when I pair something mundane with something empowering. For example, when I'm making breakfast and preparing the kids' lunches in the morning I have my laptop out. I plug in my little speaker, and I listen to podcasts that are going to help me move toward my goals. While you're driving to work, you might have a CD set that offers great sales training. This is a time for you to do some personal development and continue to learn and empower yourself.

When you sit down to work during the time you've blocked off for your goals, engage in activities that will bring you the greatest return on your investment of time and bring you more momentum as you speed closer to the finish line.

CREATE SPACE

"You have to let go of what's in your hand to reach out for something new."

~ Sonia Choquette

According to Aristotle, "Nature abhors a vacuum." Because of the laws of nature and physics, empty or unfilled spaces are unnatural. Nature requires every space to be filled with something, even if that something is colorless, odorless air. I am constantly conducting scientific experiments to test this theory with our kitchen table. We start the day with it completely cleared off. All the items that accumulated there the day before have been removed from the table and put in their proper places. However, by the end of the day that table is filled with papers, the kids' crayons, dishes, and other odds and ends again. It happens every single day! It's law! While glancing at the pile of stuff, Joe and I shake our heads and simply say, "Well, nature **does** abhor a vacuum!" The empty area sucks in everything it can at the Gleason household.

You can apply this scientific truth to your goal achievement processes. You can take action by cleaning out the old and making room for the new because nature will have to fill that space with something. When you create that empty space, you invite the new to come into your life. So, get out some garbage bags, boxes, and even the broom so you can begin to sift through the clutter in your life!

Clean every day.

An activity I often assign to the members of my group coaching program is to clean something every day. The question that I want you to ask yourself is, "What do I need to let go of that no longer serves me?" Look around you first, in your physical space. Take five minutes and tidy up your desk, clean out that junk drawer, sift through your glove box, or rearrange a shelf in a cupboard. Go through your closet and get rid of the items you no longer wear. Make room and watch how fast new things are going to fill those empty spaces in your life.

Moving beyond your physical environment, you can also clean up the intangible. One of my corporate clients shared with me that as his team became super focused about their department goals, they committed all of their efforts to attaining them. Many things changed regarding their action, but interestingly enough, they cleaned up their schedules. He told me how they made room for extra time to work toward their goals by canceling business trips, meetings, and other unnecessary events. This opened up room in their days for rallying the troops and innovating solutions, which was key to their smashing success!

What can you let go of today? Start sifting through the clutter and throw away the unneeded so nature can fill that space with the new opportunities, resources, and ideas that will ultimately lead you to crossing the finish line.

Make a container.

When looking to bring something new into your life, create a container, a bucket, to make room for the new. Remember, it's a law of nature that this empty space will want to be filled. Declare your intention for what you want to go into that space. During The Big Drive, we sold our minivan to make room in the garage for the

Camaro. That's how far we went to make room for the grand prize in my life.

Here are some ideas to get you thinking about a new container you can open:

- Open a new bank account to collect money for your vacation or for your new business venture.
- Buy a desk and set up the space for the new employee you are looking to hire.
- Purchase the domain name for your new website.
- Create a new folder on your computer desktop and label it with the name of your project or the title of your book.
- Clear off a space on the shelf where you will place the trophy or medal when you win it!
- Reserve time in your schedule each week to teach that new class.
- Create a chart with open slots for the names of your new clients. Write the names as you acquire them.

Lara, a member of my Achieve online program hired me for a few private coaching sessions as she was looking to grow her business by creating a niche as a consultant for women business coaches. I assigned her the task to make a poster containing a list of the qualities she desired in her new clients (her "Mary Poppins List") and a chart divided into six sections. Each section represented a space for a new client.

After creating the chart, she added the name of her one existing client that fit the criteria and hung the poster on the wall. She described this as "daunting and a bit nerve-wracking" at first having five empty slots to fill, but Lara focused and began to use this chart daily as she looked for new clients. During a follow up call she described her experience, "When I was on the phone speaking to a potential client, I would glance at it and remind myself the client needed to fit into my criteria to qualify. As the chart began to fill, I was able to let go of a few less than ideal clients." Lara's goal was to fill all six slots by September 1, but by July 1, the chart was full and her practice was thriving with six of her ideal clients!

It's your turn to make a container to hold the new experience you wish to create, just like Lara did. Create a new empty container, whether it's a chart, a bucket, or fresh clean space in your life and fill it with what you desire.

Tie up loose ends.

Do you have any unfinished business in your life? Is there something that needs to get wrapped up before you can achieve this new goal? When you tie up any loose ends in your life, you create space for more time, support, and progress toward your goals.

If your goal is to create a new website, start by doing a little clean-up of your old website. Make a few tweaks here and there so it doesn't need your attention. Then, you can focus on developing the content for your new website. Let's say that your goal is to launch a new information product, such as an online course, audio program, or DVD series. Finish up an existing project. While working on this book, I realized I had some unfinished business I needed to tend to. I wanted to make my online program, Achieve, a self-study course. I rallied my pit crew and took a week to finish up what I had been procrastinating to do. I recorded the new welcome video. We uploaded transcripts and added some fast track learning points to aid the self-learner. Once that was finished, I felt relieved. I didn't realize the pressure that the course had caused me. Once I checked that off of my "to-do" list, I was able to move on and really focus on my book!

The clean-up doesn't even need to be directly related to your goals. Work on finishing your house cleaning, getting that scrapbook done, or going through the pile of bills and junk mail. Give yourself a purpose or a deadline and make it fun! If you still haven't completely unpacked after your move, plan a housewarming party. You'll get your new place in tip-top shape in time for the event, and then, get to enjoy the fruits of your labor with your friends and family. Schedule a scrapbooking gathering with some of your friends. Have everybody bring their tools and supplies so you can all share with each other. Hold each other accountable for getting things done, and of course, "Whistle while you work!" Instead of dreading the chore of going through the basket of junk mail, change it up a bit. What if you approached the task in a different way? Expect a surprise! The last time I went through the pile of unopened mail, I found $500 in checks, gift cards, and cash!

Do whatever it takes to clean up your unfinished business. Get the help you need to tie up any loose ends so you can move onto your next endeavor. Once you eliminate the distractions, you will be able to focus on the road ahead.

Let go of the past.

Sometimes there are circumstances from your past that you haven't let go of yet. Maybe you were wronged in some way or somebody hurt you years and years ago. This may be keeping you from moving forward. Is there something that you need to let go of that no longer serves you? When you stop feeling angry or resentful toward another person, a situation, or even with yourself, you can open up the space to move forward in life. Forgiveness is not always easy, but it will set you free when you are able to let go of the blame.

Once you've identified that you are holding on to old baggage, haven't let go of something from your past, or have a victim mentality, make plans to take a reflective walk, a hike, or even take a pilgrimage if you are called to do so. Choose a destination and take that walk silently. Leave your cell phone, iPod, and any other distractors behind. This is time for you to think, reflect, and decide on what you need to forgive.

During the writer's retreat in Sedona with Pamela and Betsy, we took a field trip: a light hike along the Bell Rock Pathway, trails at the beautiful red rock formation. As we rode the bus to the location, they asked us to be completely silent. They posed two questions, asking us to reflect on them during our hike: What will you leave here and what will you take with you? This was a powerful and transformational experience for me. The first portion of the walk seemed daunting. As I walked along the rough terrain, I noticed the sharp needles of the paddle cactus alongside the rocky path. These needles represented the various sources of pain, hardships, and losses in my life. As I continued down the path, I glanced at dead branches, fallen tree trunks, and rotting plant life. These all represented the old me, the failures and anger I wanted to leave behind.

When it was time to sit and reflect at the base of Bell Rock, I had a really hard time quieting my mind so I decided to focus on what was directly in front of me. I noticed a little plant with tiny purple flowers. I imagined each bud being one of my beloved readers, and each had the potential to become something beautiful: to bloom into a pretty, happy, and full flower. I realized I needed to nurture this plant, keep it protected, and give it what it needed to bloom. This was my purpose: to write a book that would help others grow and achieve their full potential.

As we hiked back, something changed and no longer did I notice the dead, dark, pieces in nature. Instead, I saw the thriving plant life and beautiful colors of nature all around me. Instead of seeing dead trees, I saw the most vibrant green leaves and new growth all around me. I looked up and saw the magnificent red rock formations against a clear blue sky. It was during the last portion of my hike that I decided to take with me a new commitment to this book, to write, and to empower others to fulfill their purpose and achieve their goals. That's what I took with me. I left the old behind and had a renewed purpose and passion to help others.

Try journaling after your walk to realize the old pieces of you that you're leaving behind and feel inspired about what you're taking with you. Your new goals, your new passions. The act of writing will release the unwanted burden and allow you to focus on your future.

Get help if you need it. Seek professional counseling or coaching to assist you with being able to forgive. Reconcile with others, resolve the problem or situation, and allow yourself to forgive and let go. Put the past behind you in order to focus on the present and look forward to the future.

Avoid negativity.

Another type of action to take is to avoid negativity in your life. My husband and I tell our kids that, "You become like the people you hang out with," and "If you want to be successful, you need to hang out with successful people." If you hang out with the wrong crowd, they're going to bring you down. Is there a partnership that is just making you feel terrible and not allowing you to move forward and have joy in your life? Maybe you need to spend less time with a certain person that makes you feel agitated. Is there a negative person on your team or in your company that needs to go so that you can move forward? Be selective about your time and who you spend it with.

What needs to go so you can make room for the new and have time to work toward your new goals? Who and what is standing in the way of your dreams? Again, it's time to put the pedal to the metal, put your nose to the grindstone, and get to work. As you take massive action, you'll head as fast as you can toward that finish line. Feel the rush of excitement and passion as everything unfolds in front of you!

 ## GET INTO GEAR

- Hit the gas and be prepared to work harder than you ever have before.
- Create your "to-do" list and prioritize your action items to stay on track.
- Put together a schedule to make time to dedicate to your goals.
- Show up and stay committed to your goals daily.
- Punch through your "to-do" list and work on your goals every day, even if it is in small chunks of time.
- Clean out the old to make room for the new.
- Tie up loose ends and avoid negativity in your life.

 ## ACCELERATE TOWARD YOUR SUCCESS

1. Create your "to-do" list for your goals and begin to prioritize what needs to get done first. Block off time each day for focused action and work through your list. Don't forget to reward yourself for a job well done!

2. Clear out the clutter in your life by taking to time to clean something. Then, make a container to hold the achievement of your goals. It could be an actual box or space for the items. It could also be symbolic like a chart on a piece of paper that you can fill in with the names of your new clients.

ON THE ROAD REFLECTIONS

In your journal, take some time to write a letter to someone you wish to reconcile with. How has that person wronged you or hurt you in the past? Share your feelings and tell how that situation has impacted you. Then, write about your forgiveness. Release yourself and the other person from that situation. Let it go so you can move forward in the direction of your dreams.

**Put your motivation into overdrive and
head as fast as you can toward the finish line!**

AVOID OBSTACLES ALONG THE ROAD

**"The road less traveled is sometimes fraught with
barricades, bumps, and unchartered terrain. But it is on
that road where your character is truly tested."**

~ Katie Couric

When a race car driver enters a race, he or she knows there's potential for disaster. What good is a race without the excitement of the strategy, the thrill of avoiding the obstacles, or the skill of avoiding that crash? You chose goals that would challenge you and get you to the next level. I can guarantee you it won't be all "teddy bears, unicorns, ice cream, and a bowl of cherries." You might be faced with obstacles, detours, smash-ups, and dead ends. Throughout this process, worry and doubt are going to creep in and try to destroy your plans. Learn how to eliminate your obstacles by managing your fear. Be prepared with strategies that can help you bypass these roadblocks so that you can keep your eye on the prize!

BUMPS IN THE ROAD

For me, the road to winning the Camaro was not an easy one. I took massive action, and I worked countless hours. I was tested and confronted with obstacles that would make me step up, face my fears, and admit my shortcomings. All the while, I made it a point to be completely aware of my emotions and feelings, using them as indicators for my progress on my path to victory. I made a concerted effort to always keep my eye on the prize and stay focused on crossing the finish line as the grand prize winner of a new Camaro.

During my journey I avoided many obstacles, but I also had to meet some of them head on. Sometimes I found myself crashed up, burned out, or even stuck in a pothole. That's when I turned to my support network, my biggest fans, my coaches and mentors, and even my subconscious mind, to help me get back on track. Because I took so much action with this massive workload of creating programs, servicing customers, and having a new team to manage, I found it extremely overwhelming at times. I had to manage my stress. I did that by making sure that I built in "me time" where I could rest and rejuvenate so I had the energy to keep moving forward.

I felt like I was going in reverse when my rank on the leaderboard dropped a couple of notches or a problem faced me straight on. Sometimes if I had no solution available to me, I began to feel doubt. I would even think, "Do I really have what it takes to win? I'm up against the best of the best in sales in this contest." I had to clear those thoughts by repeating my affirmations. I would repeat over and over again, "I've got what it takes to win. I am a success. I am a winner." That would make me feel more confident, and I'd think of how I could take steps toward my goal.

At times, I got really discouraged. My sales skyrocketed at the beginning of the contest. I came out of the gates on fire. I sold 25 software subscriptions in only two weeks. I was already halfway to my goal of 50, and nobody even saw me coming. I got shout outs on Facebook from my colleagues and friends. I was invited to go to Infusionsoft's headquarters for an interview to share my selling secrets with others. But during the next several weeks, I was so busy creating and fulfilling these programs that I didn't have time to sell. As I watched the leaderboard being updated every day, I began to panic as my competitors inched closer and closer to me. I could feel them breathing down my neck. I started thinking that I needed a miracle. I worried that there wasn't enough time to keep my solid lead in front of the others, but I kept plugging along and taking action every day.

There were days where I allowed myself to think, "Well, Janette, even if you don't win the car, you're really doing a great job. Look at all that you've done. Second or third place would be okay. It would be awesome, and you could settle for that." No sooner did those words enter my mind that I pushed them right back out, saying, "No, I am number one this time. I am driving home in the Camaro."

I also suffered from feeling guilty during the contest. I felt sorry that I was beating the others. This is something that I have always struggled with. Watching someone else lose is really hard on me, and I often let up during a contest or game because I hate to see others disappointed and frustrated with themselves. I realized that one of my strengths, having empathy, can actually be a huge weakness for me, especially in a competitive environment. I understand and share the feelings of others, which I knew was going to hold me back in this contest. I reached out to my coach for guidance. I told her how I'd always been this way and how sometimes I ease up just to let others win. She told me to mind my own business! She said, "Janette, just worry about you right now. It's about your growth, your goals, and your path." This advice gave me permission to feel I deserved being number one in the end.

My biggest fear during The Big Drive was losing. After all, I made these bold declarations about winning the car, and I started to fear that worst-case scenario, that I would lose. I imagined being mocked, being laughed at, disappointing my family, and the embarrassment that I would feel. It was all in my head though. I was painting pictures in my mind of something that wasn't even true! That's why my visualizations were so powerful. I looked forward to the time every night when I tucked myself into bed, put my headphones on, and listened to my meditation. It was not just about getting to that place where I could visualize every detail of my victory. It was also about seeing myself share this amazing accomplishment with others: my family, my friends, and my colleagues. It was my deep feeling of gratitude that actually catapulted me right over this massive brick wall that I called fear.

When I became aware of my weaknesses, it was the key to overcoming them. If you don't know it's a problem for you, then you can't fix it. It's not fun to experience problems and detours along your journey, but it's when you're able to overcome them that the real growth and transformation can occur. This is what gets you to the next level, in your business, in your career, or in your personal life. This is what it's all about. It's about challenging yourself, doing something new, and growing. So when you can, acknowledge that there is a problem or that you have a weakness and use it to your advantage.

Learn how to navigate around the potholes, know when you need to stop for help and refuel when necessary. After a crash, stop for repairs and get right back into the race. Most importantly, stay in the running toward your goals!

IDENTIFY YOUR OBSTACLES

The first step to bypassing or eliminating your roadblocks is to identify them! What is in your way? What is the problem you face at the moment? During my private coaching calls, when I can sense there has been a setback or I hear frustration in my client's voice, I'll ask the question, "What's the biggest obstacle you're facing right now?" I get lots of answers:

- There's fierce competition. I see the other people in the running and how talented they are, and I don't know how I can measure up.

- The deadline is nearing quickly. I feel like I'm running out of time.

- I don't have enough money or other resources to get the job done.

- I'm making slow progress toward my goal. I feel like I'm taking action, but I'm not getting anywhere.

- Something happened that was out of my control, and it's just not fair!

- I made a mistake, and now I've got to start all over again.

- It seems impossible. With what I can see in front of me, I don't know how I'm going to be able to get there. I just don't see how this will come together.

After my client identifies the obstacle, my next question is "How do you feel about it?" Okay, so you've got this competitor, there's this deadline, or you've got to start all over; how does that make you feel? Because it's really not the obstacle that's going to keep you from achieving your goals. It's how you're feeling and reacting to those feelings that's going to hold you back.

Take some time to reflect and identify your obstacles. After you do, check in with your feelings. Keep in mind that you create with your thoughts, your images, and your actions, but your feelings are actually the indicators of your progress. Right now, it's your job to get yourself back to a state of belief, enthusiasm, passion, and joy, as soon as possible. A bad day is bound to happen now and again. Maybe it's even a really bad day where you're angry, frustrated, or overwhelmed. That's all right. Feel it, acknowledge it, and then work to change it. You have control over your feelings, so do whatever you can to feel better.

Once you identify your obstacle and how it makes you feel, you can begin to seek solutions:

- Consult with your coach for guidance when you are discouraged.
- Spend time with your family to ease your worries.
- Head to the gym to alleviate the stress you feel.
- Watch a funny movie when you are bored.
- Make a plan so you feel more confident.
- Squeeze a stress ball when you feel aggravated.
- Ask for help when you are overwhelmed.
- Call up your BFF to help raise your spirits when you feel insecure.

Avoiding or eliminating obstacles is really about feeling good, staying strong, and keeping focused on the results, on that outcome, that you want. It's about leaning on your team, the people you've assembled to support you throughout this journey. Throughout the book, you've been learning strategies to help you achieve your goals. You have all these tools in your tool belt now, and you're learning when to pick them up and use them.

MANAGE WORRY AND FEAR

Fear is the absolute lowest level on the Emotional Guidance Scale and worry isn't far behind it. During The Big Drive, I felt threatened that the other competitors would pass me up. I worried that my prospects would tell me no. I felt anxiety when I thought that some customers would cancel their subscriptions, causing me to lose credit for the sales. I feared coming in as runner-up in the contest and that all of my hard work would be for nothing in the end. I conjured up these stories in my mind and imagined all of these horrible things happening. I knew I needed to stop them dead in their tracks. I remembered the sayings, "What you think about, you bring about," and "What you fear comes upon you." I didn't want these made up thoughts to come true. I had to bust through the massive brick wall in front of me if I wanted to win.

Letting yourself wallow in fear is such a horrible and detrimental place to be. Being afraid of the unknown and worrying about what **might** happen can actually cause people to back out and abandon their goals. They throw their hands up in the air and say, "I'm out of here!" Don't let worry or fear get in the way of your dreams. Stop dwelling on the difficulties or troubles in your path. Instead, find solutions and focus on navigating through the bumpy spots.

Here are some tips to help you manage your worry and fear:

Ask yourself, "Is it true?"

Thoughts that come into your mind, making you feel fear or doubt can keep you from achieving your goals. When you begin to have fear about the unknown or start to worry about a situation, remember...it's the unknown! I've seen an acronym for F.E.A.R., which represents:

False

Evidence

Appearing

Real

When you are faced with the unknown and it causes you anxiety, ask yourself, "Is it true?" Many times you'll see that it's only something you're making up as a possibility. It hasn't actually occurred and isn't really an imminent danger for you. There's time and the opportunity to find a solution. Byron Katie, author and creator of *The Work* teaches a method of identifying and questioning thoughts that cause fear or other negative feelings such as anger or depression.

Here are the four questions Byron Katie suggests you ask yourself:

1. Is it true?
2. Can you absolutely know that it's true?
3. How do you react, what happens, when you believe that thought?
4. Who would you be without the thought?

By asking yourself these questions, you can experience the opposite of what you believe, simply by changing your thoughts. Try managing your fear this way. You may just realize the boogie man under your bed is just a figment of your imagination! There may be a better thought there for you, one that is the truth you would prefer.

I used this process by recommendation of my business coach, Pamela Slim. During a call with her, I felt some anxiety about taking my business in a new direction. After The Big Drive, I had a taste of executive coaching. I realized how much I loved it and that I could do it all day, every day. Pam could tell something was bothering me, so I said, "I'm feeling really frustrated with myself. Here I am again with new ideas to pursue. Pam, I have these other projects that I've been working on, but now I want to start all over again and go in a different direction. Why am I always seeking something new and different? How can I be successful if I can't focus? I never stick with anything!"

After I got all of that out, she asked me, "Janette, is that true? Is it true that you never stick with anything?" I closed my mouth for a moment so I could think. No, it wasn't true. In fact, there were many things I had stuck with: my marriage, our financial planning business, longtime friends. What I had been telling myself about never sticking with anything was not the truth. I realized that I was committed to teaching, empowering, and inspiring others, and how that's the common thread in any work that I do. Even though my products and services may change, I'm always committed to learning, growing, and sharing that knowledge with others. I may veer in a different direction, but my purpose remains the same. These new thoughts and beliefs felt much better. The fear of my uncertainty to head in a new direction subsided. I felt more confident than ever that I was headed on the right path.

> **"Stand up to your obstacles and do something about them, you will find that they haven't half the strength that you think they have."**
> ~ Norman Vincent Peale

Stand up to your fears and worries. Having lived much of my life as a perpetual worrier, I have projected all sorts of scenarios that hadn't actually occurred yet: from grades on tests, to getting the job I applied for, to paying all the bills. My mind has the uncanny ability to imagine the worst! This tendency has resulted in me being overwhelmed with anxiety and even suffering from panic attacks at one point. I knew I needed to manage my worries so I could live a more peaceful, happier life.

I realized that when I worry, I'm really only afraid of what might happen. I discovered a process to help me manage and eliminate my worry:

- Identify what you are worried about. Say what you're afraid of and acknowledge it. When you start to worry, ask yourself "What am I really afraid of here?"

- Describe the worst-case scenario. So what? What's the worst thing that can happen if what you're worrying about comes true?

- Now put a positive spin on it. How could this actually benefit you? What would be the gold you could discover from going through this experience?

During The Big Drive, I worried about my competitors. There were others in the running who were, and still are, extremely successful salesmen. In fact, I knew one of them had a real knack for coming in at the very end of a contest, selling a massive amount, and crushing the competition. I could feel it coming and my fear was, "He's going to sell a ton of software subscriptions, and I am going to lose my lead!" I decided to use my three-step process. I asked myself, "Okay, what is the worst-case scenario if he did? I wouldn't be in the lead anymore so I would need to step up, get creative, and sell more. Then, I thought about how I could put a positive spin on this. I told myself that by pushing myself to sell more, I'd be helping more people. More business owners would benefit from purchasing Infusionsoft and implementing my campaigns. In the end, I would feel even prouder about what I had achieved.

Let's imagine that your goal is to move into your dream house. You might be worried about the bank approving your loan because it is a larger mortgage than you have right now, and you've had some credit blemishes during recent years. Sitting around worrying about something that is out of your control for the moment will not bring you closer to your goal. Keeping your thoughts on the outcome —your Celebratory Moment— will. To do that, you may need to stand up to the thoughts that have been bullying you. Ask yourself, "What is the worst-case scenario?" The bank rejects the application for your loan. Not ideal, but now you have identified a problem you can fix. They might tell you to satisfy a delinquent account and pay down some debt. Get to work on taking care of those items, and you'll come out even better on the other side! The positive spin will be better credit, lower credit card payments, and the approved loan for the house of your dreams!

There is no use sitting around and worrying. Be strong and face your fears. Empower yourself by implementing this process and release the anxiety you feel about your roadblocks.

Say the Ho'oponopono Prayer.
Ho'oponopono means "to make things right." This beautiful Hawaiian prayer allows you to release fear and negativity in your life.

There are four simple sentences in this prayer:

I love you.
I'm sorry.
Please forgive me.
Thank you.

Think about all the positive feelings that are expressed in this prayer: love, forgiveness, and gratitude. These feelings are at the very top of the Emotional Guidance Scale. I have made it a habit to repeat this prayer throughout my day. I say it upon waking, before a coaching call with a client, as I sit down to a meal, or even while I'm waiting at a stoplight. I will also say this prayer if I have a problem or face a situation where I'm feeling a little uncomfortable. I've said this prayer and things that I thought were going to be major problems just completely dissipated and were a non-issue. It has done miracles for me.

I remember one day I felt a bit nervous before a call with a customer. I thought the customer was unsatisfied, and I was not looking forward to the call. I didn't know how that other person was going to react, and I anticipated a possible confrontation, which made me feel uneasy. Before I picked up the phone, I prayed, "I love you, I'm sorry, please forgive me, thank you." Immediately that brought me to a better feeling place. During the call, the customer was extremely pleasant. We had a great talk and came to a compromise that suited us both! No fuss, no muss!

To eliminate obstacles along the road, relax, let go, and say the Ho'oponopono Prayer to remove fear and worry.

Bless Your Mess.

Say "Thank you." Say it always and often, and actually feel it. Gratitude is one of the highest vibrations. Empower yourself by expressing gratitude for the obstacles in your way, because they are going to help you identify the weaknesses you need to overcome. Bless the problem, be grateful for your competitors, and thank your adversaries.

Say:

- *Thank you for doing your job.*
- *Thank you for making me stronger.*
- *Thank you for making me work harder.*
- *Thank you for making me change and grow.*
- *I'm so thankful that I can identify that I have empathy and that this is what's keeping me from being number one.*

- *I'm thankful for my competitor, that he's pushing me farther than I ever thought I could go, and I'm grateful for that.*

If there is a problem in your way, the best thing is just to be thankful for it. When you bless your mess, you will go from feeling powerless to feeling empowered, ready to tackle the obstacles ahead of you. Sometimes the obstacle, that boulder in the middle of your path can seem so massive, but all you need to do is face it and figure out a way around it.

> **"Develop an attitude of gratitude, and give thanks for everything that happens to you, knowing that every step forward is a step toward achieving something bigger and better than your current situation."**
>
> ~ Brian Tracy

DOUBT BUSTERS

Doubt is a sneaky little devil. It can creep in when you least expect it! In Chapter 2 you worked so hard to get to a state of belief regarding your goals, so don't let doubt come in and pester you with thoughts like:

- *You're not good enough to live in that house.*
- *There can't be a solution. Nobody has ever done this before.*
- *Oh, you don't have enough time! The deadline is nearing and the clock is ticking.*
- *You'll never be able to publish a book! That's way too hard.*
- *You don't deserve to win that contest. Who do you think you are?*

Chris, the senior manager of The Getting Started Team at Infusionsoft, was working toward his department's goals one quarter and had participated in one of my workshops where he created an Achieve Box. After decorating the sides of the box and placing "I Believe" statements inside of it, he set it on his desk. Chris explained how he used the box daily as a reminder to check in with his belief. Each day, he glanced at the box and asked himself the question, "Am I in belief today?" After carefully examining his feelings, if the thought was, "no," he'd asked himself, "Why?" Maybe it was a hard day. Maybe he missed the mark, or he didn't do what he set out to do that day. But then he switched to thinking about solutions, "How can I get back to a state of belief?" Chris used strategies such as meditation to help clear his mind and get back to belief.

Are you in belief today or are you in doubt today? It is inevitable that doubt will try to sneak in and derail your plans. Work to obliterate it with these simple techniques:

1. If an apprehensive thought enters your mind, simply say, "No, go away!" and push it out of your mind. Retrain your subconscious mind to think more positively by being simple and direct (and repeat if necessary).

2. Try this visualization: Imagine you have blinders on and that the doubt or the negative thought is now out of your sight. Turn your attention and focus straight ahead to the finish line where you have achieved your goals. Every moment, you're stepping just a little bit closer to that line.

3. If you feel overwhelmed, take a few moments and get centered. All you need to do is close your eyes and begin to focus on your breathing. As you breathe in and breathe out, direct your thoughts to the visions of your Celebratory Moment. This will help you start to feel better instantly. When the worry subsides, you can move on with your day.

4. Repeat your mantra. Earlier, you selected a snappy slogan or phrase. During periods of doubt, you can say it out loud, read it, and repeat it. Your mantra is a simple tool you can use to eradicate doubt quickly.

5. Another tool that I use when doubt creeps in or when I'm confronted with a new problem is to repeat a simple sentence. I close my eyes and say, "I trust everything will work out." I'll say it aloud to myself or to anyone one else around me. Immediately, I get to a better feeling place.

6. You can also play a game called "Wouldn't it be nice if …" I learned about this activity in Esther Hick's book, *Ask and It Is Given*. When you are confronted with doubt and you have difficulty thinking of solutions to a problem you face, try playing this game with another person. Take turns going back and forth by beginning your phrase with, "Wouldn't it be nice if…" and then, fill in the blank with a pleasant solution to your issue.

Example:

You and your partner have set a goal to move to a new house, but you find yourselves worrying about the logistics of how it's all going to happen. Take turns presenting positive outcomes such as:

- *Wouldn't it be nice if we were able to sell our house quickly?*
- *Wouldn't it be nice if the transition went smoothly?*
- *Wouldn't it be nice if our loan is approved without a snag?*
- *Wouldn't it be nice if the owners of the new house were pleasant to deal with?*
- *And wouldn't it be nice if the timing worked out perfectly?*

Keep going back and forth with the other person until you both feel better and more excited about the possible solutions to your problems. Get over the doubt and move on to the next step of your journey to success.

DEAD ENDS, DETOURS, AND CRASHES

"Every adversity, every failure, every heartache, carries with it the seed of an equal or greater benefit."

~ Napoleon Hill

When faced with adversity, do you give up and abandon your dreams? Successful people stay committed and steadfast to their goals. They learn from their mistakes, their failures, and their hardships. Your obstacles can be turning points for you. Adversity might appear just to move you in the right direction or to delay things until that right moment when everything comes into alignment for you.

What are the obstacles you may face during your race to the finish?

- The inspection goes terribly and the dream house that you thought you were going to live in doesn't work out.
- Your employee quits and nobody else knows where to pick up on that major project.
- Your car breaks down and the money you were saving for your flight to Italy is completely depleted.
- You lose your biggest client and hitting your revenue goals seems next to impossible.
- The loan is not approved for starting your brand-new business.

Some of the biggest obstacles that we've faced as a family have been major turning points, defining moments, in our lives. A few years back, my husband's office manager quit suddenly. At the time, it seemed like the end of the world to lose our key employee, and it was a huge setback to overcome. In hindsight, it was actually a blessing in disguise. This unexpected event brought me into the office where I learned about marketing, and I started using Infusionsoft to automate our processes. We doubled our revenue during tax season that year, which brought us closer to our business goals. Upon further reflection after all these years, the incident launched a new career path for me and brought me to where I am today.

One of the worst days for me was the day we lost our home. Going through foreclosure was emotionally and financially draining. The feeling of failure set in. I was angry. I grieved. And, I felt ashamed. Having to pick up the pieces of the mess we were in, we packed up our things and moved into a little rental house to make a fresh start. While it was excruciating to go through this traumatic experience, we realized that it was the best thing for our family. It freed us from our massive mortgage payment and the debt that was choking us every month. Getting through that obstacle together brought us closer to each other and paved the way to bigger and better things for our family. Our new beginning allowed us to move forward and grow our business in ways we never imagined.

When you smash into a wall or crash and burn, it's a true test of your faith. Will you get back up and keep going? You break through a crisis or period of struggle by taking any of the following actions:

1. Accept 100% responsibility for where you are. Don't waste your energy pointing the finger at somebody else and playing the victim card. That will not get you anywhere. When you claim ownership of your situation, you take control and empower yourself to make things better.

2. Pick yourself up and start over. Wise words from Vince Lombardi tell us, "It's not whether you get knocked down, it's whether you get up." True champions don't give up! They keep trying and stay committed to their goals.

3. Seek guidance and look for a new solution. When you are struggling, lean on your support network to lift you back up and help you navigate through the difficult times.

4. Be persistent. Keep asking until you get the answer or solution you are looking for.

5. Have faith! Trust that all you desire is within your reach. Have the belief that something good is waiting for you just around the corner.

Look at your dead ends, detours, and crashes as learning lessons or as turning points for you. I know it's not easy to admit your faults, own up to your weaknesses, or overcome adversity. But, when you are successful at navigating around your obstacles, you will be stronger and more empowered to accomplish things you never imagined could be possible.

GET INTO GEAR

- Identify your obstacles and check in with your feelings.
- Lean on your support network when you feel overwhelmed.
- Ask yourself if the worry and fear are true.
- Use a number of techniques including a three-step process and positive affirmations to eliminate your worry and fear.
- Bless your mess for pushing you to work harder toward your goals.
- Overcome doubt by keeping your eye on the prize, clearing your mind, and thinking of your Celebratory Moment.
- View adversity as opportunities for learning.

ACCELERATE TOWARD YOUR SUCCESS

1. Manage fear and worry by asking yourself if they are true, standing up to them and expressing gratitude for the learning opportunities they present to you.

2. When you feel doubt begin to creep in, you've got to put the brakes on it quickly. Use any of the techniques I shared in this chapter to rid your mind of doubt, starting with the need to get to a state of belief ASAP!

ON THE ROAD REFLECTIONS

What is the biggest obstacle you face right now that is keeping you from achieving your goals? What steps can you take to overcome that obstacle?

**Avoiding obstacles is really about staying strong
and keeping focused on the results you want.**

CHAPTER

9

THE HOMESTRETCH TO THE FINISH LINE

"Many of life's failures are people who
did not realize how close they were to success
when they gave up."

~ Thomas A. Edison

As you enter the final turn of your journey and head into the homestretch to the finish line, give it your all and do not give up on your dreams! You must keep a firm grasp on the steering wheel and your foot on the gas so you don't self-sabotage as you get closer to achieving your goals. Harness your energy and keep your power controlled with some simple, yet effective strategies. Maintain your winning attitude and always stay committed to your goals. You can see the checkered flag waving at the finish line!

ENTERING THE HOMESTRETCH

During the last couple of weeks of The Big Drive contest, I entered the homestretch and was neck and neck with the other top sales leaders. As I entered the final turn, I could see the finish line inching closer and closer to me, but I was exhausted physically, mentally, and emotionally. I wanted this race to be over. I wanted to wrap up this chapter of my life and get back to my normal routine. Most of all, I wanted to hold the keys to my brand-new car.

At this point, I had lost my lead. It wasn't by much, but it was enough to leave me feeling discouraged. I didn't like that my name no longer sat in that number one spot on the leaderboard. It drove me to take action once more. I reached out to all of my hot prospects. I even wrote the names of these leads on sticky notes and put them on a poster. I set that out where I could see the names and focus on them daily. My sales had gone from large numbers at a time to just single transactions here and there. I approached my partners to let them know I was ready for a new batch of customers, but they weren't ready to send them to me. That well was dry, but I didn't lose hope. I realized I had two options:

1. I could let up on the gas and just cruise over the finish line, not worrying about how I placed and being proud of what I had already accomplished.

2. I could give it all I had and continue reaching for the grand prize and be the first to cross the finish line.

During a session with my mentor, Sonia, I told her I felt like I was losing ground. I described how my mind was swirling, and I didn't know what to do with the pressure I felt as I got closer to the end of the contest. I told her about my past failures, and I realized that I had this perpetual habit of giving up just before the end. The pressure would take over me. I'd throw my hands up in the air and back out just short of reaching my goal. I did this when I was one of the top three finalists in the Ultimate Marketer contest a couple years prior to The Big Drive. I didn't want to watch that movie again. This time, I had my sights set on being victorious and taking home the grand prize.

Luckily, Sonia told me there was an easy fix. She explained the reason I short-circuited in the past: I wasn't grounding my energy. I'd get a surge of excitement that was too hard for me to contain and it would dance around like a live wire. She explained that electricity has to be grounded to light a city. In the same way, I needed to connect and channel my energy so I wouldn't implode at the end. She had me practice a visualization technique where I imagined my feet being rooted into the ground, just like that of a large oak tree. This would help me stay grounded and harness this extra energy I contained. I focused on this imagery. It really helped me get to a calmer place and to control my surplus of energy.

One afternoon, all the extra stress got to me. I was trying so hard, working so diligently, focusing my time and attention on my sales, and feeling frustrated that they were just not coming in despite all of my efforts. I decided that a dip in the pool with my family was just what I needed to give my mind a rest. As my biggest fan, my husband, Joe, is a terrific supporter of me. He always encourages me to go after my dreams and always cheers me on, especially throughout The Big Drive. As Joe and I enjoyed frosty margaritas while lazily floating around the pool, I told him about my troubles. After a bit of contemplation, he suggested that we make one of my partners an offer they simply couldn't refuse. Bingo! That was it! I knew at that moment that Joe had given me the golden idea, the one that would end up being my ticket to victory! It was when I stepped away from my computer, my desk, the phone, and all of the emails and played, that the idea "dropped in," just like Albert Einstein said it would. The next day I reached out, made the call, and the new customers began to line up. It took some time to gather that list, prepare my team, and keep these new sales in my back pocket for the very last stretch of the contest.

Mentally and emotionally, the phase during the final week was **the** most challenging time for me. I have to admit that I was a complete wreck. The stress level was overwhelming for me, almost debilitating. My stomach was in knots as I thought, "What do the others have in store?" Just as I had a strategy, did they have one, too? What cards were they holding? Was anyone bluffing? I felt really lonely, and I didn't know who I could trust. I kept really quiet during that time, and I continued to practice my oak tree visualization. Each day, I imagined my feet being rooted deeply into the ground, feeling strong and supported.

I also watched a clip from one of my favorite movies. At the end of the first *Matrix* movie, Neo discovers he is "the one." Whenever I felt out of control, I would imagine myself as Neo holding up my hand and saying, "No." The bullets flying toward me were my fears, my doubts, my problems, my shortcomings, and my insecurities, I imagined I had control over them, just as Neo did—stopping the bullets with his bare hand—and that would keep these bullets from hitting me. It was very empowering. During that final battle with his enemies, Neo realizes it's all a game. Finally, we see Neo standing with his feet completely grounded, his head lowered and his fists clenched as he takes a deep breath. During the competition when the energy was overwhelming for me, I would watch this clip. I would stand in the same way, and I would inhale slowly, breathing in strength and peace. This helped me feel the power, the strength, and the control that was going to carry me over the finish line.

The last day of the contest fell during Labor Day weekend. I had until midnight to process my sales, the ones I secretly kept in my back pocket. To help pass the time and to keep my mind wandering too far off from the straight and narrow, we invited our friends, family, and even some of my team members over for a barbeque and pool party. We had bottles of champagne chilling in the refrigerator along with party hats and blowers for the big midnight finish. In a way, I felt as though I was in the running for political office. I had all my supporters there to rally around me and to anticipate the victory together. I planned to celebrate that night one way or another, but I held the image that I would be toasting to my big win.

Throughout the day we played a game of selecting songs to keep our moods elevated and our spirits high: "The Final Countdown," "Simply The Best," and "Eye Of The Tiger" were just a few on the playlist. My final strategy was to wait until 11 p.m., one hour before the contest deadline, to begin processing my last group of sales. The thought ran through my mind, "Do I have enough?" I released these final doubts and worries and told myself, "Janette, you worked as hard as you could and you gave it your all. There are no regrets. You've got this!"

As the clock struck 11 p.m., my friend and team member, Martha, and I sat down at the kitchen table with our laptops and the information in hand to enter my final sales. We began typing feverishly, processing the sales. My heart was pounding. This was it! Our final push to the finish line! One by one, we popped them into the computerized shopping cart. Then, suddenly my laptop froze. I still had sales to process! "Oh my goodness! Not now!" I ran yelling and screaming my way into my home office where my desktop computer was located. I fired it up and frantically called my right hand man, Cory. He stayed on the phone with me as I successfully entered the information for the final customers. The last few minutes were a whirlwind of excitement and adrenaline.

He gave me a play-by-play of what the other competitors were doing and cheered me on through my last few steps.

My last sale was still processing as the clock struck midnight. That spinning circle on the computer screen kept spinning. My thoughts were screaming, "It's still processing! Will it make it in time?" The stress was almost unbearable. Finally, I said to Cory, "It's midnight, Cory! Did it go through? Can you see the last sale?" Cory announced the final shot of his leaderboard, saying, "Janette, you did it! You are in the lead by one sale!" I blurted out, "That's it? Only one?" Cory chuckled and said, "Yeah, but all you need is one! Congratulations! You just won The Big Drive!" I sat in complete awe for a moment and felt a little bit of relief, too. I thanked Cory for all of his hard work and support throughout the entire contest and for staying up until midnight to coach me through the homestretch.

With a smile plastered on my face, I stood up and walked out of my home office. Beaming with pride, I joined my friends and family in the kitchen. They all stared at me with hopeful eyes, and I announced the great news, "We did it! We won!" Cheers, laughter, and celebratory music replaced the tension that had filled the air. Joe popped open the champagne bottles and poured some sparkling cider for the kids. We all gave each other hugs and high fives and toasted to our sweet success. With our bubbly drinks in hand and party hats on, we stood around the kitchen island. Almost as if right out of a movie, we held up our glasses and all together began to sing Queen's timeless victory song:

We are the champions, my friends,

And we'll keep on fighting 'til the end.

We are the champions.

We are the champions.

No time for losers

'Cause we are the champions... of the world!

I had passed my checkered flag and for the first time, I was the champion. My hard work had paid off. The new me was a first-place winner, and it was a moment I'll never forget. As I went to bed that night, visions of Camaros danced in my head, and I slept soundly knowing I had accomplished my big, hairy, audacious goal!

However, that's not where the story ends. It was a little dicey because there was a photo finish. I had only won by a nose! After the contest, Infusionsoft conducted an audit, checking the validity of each and every one of our sales. I had to show proof to verify my customers were legitimate. Also, those who cancelled their subscriptions during this time would not count toward my total. I couldn't announce my victory publicly or share the good news with anyone else yet, and it was really hard for me to keep this secret. It was the biggest thing I had ever accomplished, and I couldn't shout it from the rooftop!

When the auditing process was complete, I was contacted and told that the official calls were being made that day to the winners. At my scheduled time, I had my tissues on hand because I knew it would be emotional for me. When I received the call, my sales rep, Cory, was on the phone with Brian Jambor, the senior manager of partner programs. They started the conversation by telling me that it was a wonderful contest and that they appreciated my cooperation during the audit. Then, I heard the best news as they congratulated me for being the grand prize winner. I remember the relief, the joy, and the complete gratitude that I felt at that moment. For the first time in my life, I had finished in first place. I had fulfilled my dream, and I cried tears of joy. I told Cory and Brian how thankful I was for this entire experience. The next order of business was the logistics of the car. They asked me what color car I wanted, and I shouted out, "Red!" I had been listening to my theme song about a red Camaro every day for months so it was only appropriate that I requested red. They assured me they would do their best to make that wish come true.

My journey wasn't over quite yet. I had just a few more weeks until the awards ceremony when I could finally bring the car home. Each night, I continued my visualization of giving my acceptance speech and coasting along to the Winner's Circle. There was still much more to come and pleasant surprises awaited me!

A WINNING ATTITUDE

"Starting strong is good. Finishing strong is epic."

~ Robin Sharma

During your homestretch, you need to show up like you've never shown up to anything before. Stay true to your dreams and your goals, and don't abandon them. You are here to finish the race, and you're going to keep in control by staying grounded and pressing forward. Give it your all and finish strong!

One of my family's favorite television shows is *The Celebrity Apprentice*. During a past season, Leeza Gibbons earned her way into the finale as one of the final two contestants. It had come down to her and Geraldo Rivera. During this final show of the season, Donald Trump would choose the winner. He gave Leeza and her competitor one minute each to state why they deserved the coveted position as his next Celebrity Apprentice. During Leeza's turn, she expressed her joy and gratitude for the entire experience. Then, she said to Mr. Trump, "I started with my eye on the prize. I still have my eye on that prize, and I believe I am your next Celebrity Apprentice." As chills ran throughout my body, I knew Leeza was, in fact, the winner. I identified with her unwavering commitment to her goal because I shared that same drive and determination throughout The Big Drive, especially during the homestretch. I started with my eye on the prize, the Camaro, and I continued to have it the entire time. I believed that I was going to win.

Here are a few ways you can keep a winning attitude as you enter the final turn and head toward the finish:

Keep your eye on the prize. In the final stretch, you can see the finish line. Success is so close that you can imagine it as already accomplished. As you push through this final phase and give it your all, keep your eye on the prize. Look directly at the finish line and hold the image of your victory. Maintain an unwavering commitment to your goals and stay focused on the final prize.

Continue to imagine your Celebratory Moment. During the homestretch, it's critical for you to continue visualizing your Celebratory Moment before you go to sleep or when you need a moment to get focused and centered. Imagine that moment, feel it, and keep adding new details each and every time.

Expect success. Having a winning attitude is achieved by expecting success. You must believe that your success is obtainable for you. Believe it will happen and never let your positive expectations waiver. You can also make plans for what's next for you by thinking as if you've already achieved your goals.

Protect your dreams. You've planted the seeds of your desires so just like you would protect your garden, keep your dreams safe from harm. Put up a fence to keep the critters away so they don't destroy what you've grown. Pull the weeds so they don't choke and kill your plants. Be mindful and guard your goals by revisiting all of the tools and strategies in this book. Practice them until they become new habits.

Be a class act. Have a commitment to excellence in everything that you do. Being a class act means that you look to win fair and square, but it also means you need to take responsibility for your actions and think about how you're acting at any given moment. Act with integrity, be honest, and remain fair throughout your journey, and you'll rise to the top!

Do you have an unwavering commitment to your goals? Do you have a winning attitude where no one and nothing will get in your way? Stay committed. Be true to your goals. And, always keep your eye on the prize.

REMEMBER YOUR "WHY"

Sometimes while you're headed in a specific direction, you may have second thoughts. You might think that you're not on the right path, and you might consider abandoning the dream and heading back to the starting line. I tell my clients it's okay to change your plans, but you have to do it for the right reasons. First and foremost, you must check in with your feelings and make sure you're not backing out because of obstacles in your way. Do you want to turn around because you're afraid or doubting yourself? Make the effort to face your fears and overcome your doubt. You'll come out stronger on the other side! It's also important to reflect back and remember your "why." Think about when you focused on your dreams and goals and why you wrote those goals in the first place. You had a passion for these goals at one point. Contemplate what has changed and evaluate the benefits for continuing to pursue them.

A little over a year ago, I had selected the goal of writing a book, and I began to write that book. In fact, I had even written a rough draft and a book proposal for the publisher. However, I didn't have the desire to finish it. I was not at all excited to sit down and revise the book. Instead, I thought of other projects and "to-do's" to occupy my time. I even went to a writer's retreat, hoping for answers that would motivate me to complete it. For whatever reason, I lost the desire to continue even though I had already done so much work. Soon after, I decided that I had new content I was extremely excited to create. I had a new goal, a new passion to create content revolving around the 10 principles that helped me win The Big Drive. I worked on putting together a group coaching course that turned into a self-study online course. That content led to this book you are reading right now! I wasn't fearful or doubtful of my ability to write the other book, but I had temporarily lost interest in it. You see, the timing for the other book just wasn't right. It is currently on my list of things I want to complete in the future, and I know it will come into the world at just the right time!

Just as I made the decision to abandon that goal temporarily, you might run into a similar scenario. The following are some questions to ask yourself as you consider turning around and backing out:

- *Is this my true heart's desire?*
- *Am I bored? Do I need a new challenge?*
- *Is this goal still in alignment with my purpose or passion?*
- *Is the timing right? Can I revisit this at a later time?*
- *Do I have a new, more exciting goal?*
- *Is this something I need to complete? Do I need to finish this before I move on to the next goal?*

You wanted to step up and achieve more in your life so you keep going and stay the course when you can. Don't abandon your dreams! I recommend you finish what you started but sometimes it's okay to throw in the towel and go after something even bigger and better. Go with your gut!

CONTROL YOUR ENERGY

As you continue down the homestretch toward the checkered flag, it will be imperative for you to control your energy. Stay grounded so you don't short circuit or back off just before you reach the finish line. Sometimes you may feel like you're going to get zapped, self-destruct, or implode. Instead of giving up or giving in because it's too much for you to handle, try to harness it.

Here are few techniques to practice when you're feeling a surge of energy:

Exercising: Dissipate extra energy with physical activity. Move your body by doing exercise that you enjoy. Maybe it's dancing, taking a walk, going for a jog, or riding a bike. Enlist the help of a physical trainer or coach to help you push yourself even farther and to harness your energy.

Cooking and cleaning: Whenever I'm feeling overwhelmed and I don't know what to do with my extra energy, I get busy by washing dishes, peeling potatoes, or cooking something for the family. Get grounded by taking some time to prepare a nice meal for yourself, your family, or a friend. Scrubbing the floor or vacuuming are great activities, too!

Gardening: Getting grounded involves you connecting more deeply with the earth to channel the energy. You might want to consider gardening. Get your hands dirty while you plant and think about nature's process of growing life. Creating your heart's desire is like gardening: you prepare the soil, plant the seeds of your desires, nurture, and enjoy the fruits of your labor. Think about the roots of your plants settling deep into the earth.

Visualizing: Try imagining that you are connected to the center of the Earth, just as I imagined my feet were the roots of a large oak tree. Get grounded so the energy you hold matches that which is required of you to achieve your goals. This will help prevent you from short-circuiting as you near your final destination.

I call these "Get Out of Your Head" activities. It's important to intentionally get back into your body and not live in your head so much throughout the day. It's while you live and act only in your head that you think too much and create worry. When you can put down your smart phone or turn off the nonstop chatter in your mind, you will find more peace and control over your situation. Remember to dissipate the extra energy that could cause you to crash into the wall during this last stage of your race.

LET GO AND ALLOW

"Show up, do your best, and let go of the rest."

~ Leeza Gibbons

I've come to learn that letting go of control is extremely hard for me. I have a tendency to want to control every aspect of everything in my life. It's hard for me to sit around waiting for answers and to give up my control to someone else. Can you relate? Over time, I've discovered how important it is to hand it over to the universe and have faith that work is being done even when I can't see anything happening. When I'm at the point where I've done all I can do and I've put in maximum effort, I let go and allow.

While gardening, you do your work by prepping the soil, planting the seeds, watering and nurturing your plants, and keeping the weeds cleared. But, it's not you who grows the seed into the plant. The universe will grow it. You have to allow nature to take its course. You can't make it happen. You have to be patient and wait for it to grow. When it comes to manifesting your goals in your life, you must know when it's time to sit back and allow nature to do its work, too.

Try incorporating these suggestions to let go of control:

Back off and be patient. The old saying goes, "Patience is a virtue." Do you know when to sit back and wait things out? When you work to be patient, you show you have faith and complete trust that something will come to be. Having patience is something I have worked hard to achieve my entire life. I still struggle with patience from time to time because my methodical brain wants everything figured out as soon as possible. Over the years, I've learned that faith is really doing your part, your job, and all that you can, trusting that the universe is doing its job, too. When you feel you've done all you can do, let go by taking a walk, enjoying a hobby, or simply resting. Sonia Choquette says, "Doing nothing doesn't mean nothing's being done." In the pursuit of your goals, you will find that the best ideas and results come when you back off and let things happens on their own terms.

Innovate. When you are in a state of allowing, you open your mind to new ideas, more effective ways of doing things, and creative solutions. One of my corporate clients told me, "It's when my team is in a state of allowing that the innovation occurs." These new ideas and methods permanently change how we think and work, and they allow us to achieve what we once believed to be impossible. How can you allow and invite innovation? Switch things up by breaking your routine. If you always drive the same path from your home to the office, take a different route. If you always eat at the same restaurant, try a new one. Keep your eyes open to new ideas and your mind receptive to new solutions to leap over the biggest obstacles and cruise down the homestretch.

Think abundantly. When you acknowledge there is more than enough when it comes to resources available to you, you act with an abundant mindset. You know that there is an unlimited supply of air to breathe so you can think the same about things that you feel are currently lacking in your life. There is plenty of money, help, and ideas going around in this world, and you just need to know how to access these resources.

> **"Acknowledging the good that you already have in your life is the foundation for all abundance."**
> ~ Eckhart Tolle

If you suffer from feelings of scarcity, a great way to switch to a more abundant thought is to be grateful for what you already have. When you express gratitude for what you DO have, you invite more of the same into your life. Try saying:

- *I'm thankful I'm able to pay my bills today. I have more than enough money.*
- *I'm thankful for the resources I have at my disposal.*
- *I'm thankful for the time I have right now to work toward my goal.*
- *I'm thankful someone is supporting me in this endeavor. More help is on the way.*

When you are in a state of gratitude, you feel that you have more than what you need. If you still find yourself worrying about having enough, try giving that resource away to show you really are committed! That may seem counter intuitive, but when you give away your time, money, or other resources, you show faith in the abundance around you. If you feel a lack of time because of a creeping deadline, give away some of your time by volunteering. If you feel a money crunch, give a donation to a cause or organization that you believe in. If you think you don't have enough support to get the job done, reach out and help others with projects. When you give away selflessly, goodness will come back around to you.

Keep balance in your life. As you work toward a goal, it's easy to get really focused on one thing at the expense of other areas in your life. Perform a balance check to evaluate where your attention has been and which areas you may be neglecting.

For each of the following, rate your focus from 1 to 10 (with 1 being no attention at all and 10 being super focused):

- Career/Business
- Family
- Friends
- Finances
- Health/Self-care
- Social/Fun
- Personal/Spiritual Development

When you have finished rating each category, glance at the list and look for the item with the lowest score. Make it a point to attend to this area of your life and "let go" for a bit. If you've been neglecting your health, go to your local organic market, buy healthy food, and cook something delicious for dinner that nourishes your body. If you have been so focused that it's been weeks since you've been out of the house, plan a date night or a night out with your friends. Regularly block out time in your calendar to care for yourself: exercise, get regular doctor checkups, or spend the day with friends or family. Consider pampering yourself on a regular basis, too. Get a massage, go shopping, do home improvements, or anything else that brings you joy. It's when you take time to nurture yourself that you create time to reflect. This will help you allow those new ideas to drop in and will carry you to the finish line.

Your homestretch will be a combination of excitement, hard work, and perseverance as you inch closer to your victory. Remember to keep your hand on the wheel, your foot on the pedal, and your eyes looking ahead. Fuel your thoughts with your past successes and the Celebratory Moment that is just a quarter turn away.

 ## GET INTO GEAR

- Maintain your momentum so you can finish strong.
- Ground your energy so fear and doubt do not overtake your progress.
- Have a winning attitude and an unwavering commitment to your goals.
- Change your goals for the right reasons, not because of fear or doubt.
- Stay motivated by stepping away from your work and placing your attention elsewhere for a little while.
- Have faith and allow things to fall into place.
- Think abundantly and keep balance in your life.

 ## ACCELERATE TOWARD YOUR SUCCESS

1. Several times a week, undertake one or more of the grounding activities to control your energy. Scheduling these activities will refuel your mind and

body, keeping you on course toward the checkered flag.

2. Perform a balance check. I want you to do the balance check activity, looking at the different areas of your life, and assess what you've been neglecting. Then, take some time to focus on an area you've neglected. It will help you revitalize and refresh your mind and body. It will help you invite innovation into your life as you're in your homestretch.

ON THE ROAD REFLECTIONS

Protect your dreams. In Chapter 1, I asked you to write about your ideal life. What does it look like? How do you feel? I asked you to approach these questions as if you've already achieved your goals. Read through that journal entry. After you've read it, write a new entry but include more details about your life and feelings. It will be a great reminder of the progress you have made since you began the process, and it will move you into the next gear to get you past the finish line.

**During the homestretch, you are going to show up
like you've never shown up before.**

CHAPTER

**"Winners take time to relish their work,
knowing that scaling the mountain is what makes
the view from the top so exhilarating."**

~ Denis Waitley

You have crossed the finish line and made your way to victory lane! Your journey has ended, but the celebration has just begun. Line up with your team to "kiss the bricks" as the confetti cannons erupt and the crowd roars in honor of your accomplishments. Hold your head high and revel in your victory as the winner of your personal race to success. Bask in the joy of your special moment as you take your victory lap. Treasure every moment and look forward to the next race, the next finish line off in the distance. The road is wide open and there's a new green flag waving you on to the next journey.

MY VICTORY LAP

After surviving the grueling auditing process when the contest ended and receiving the call from Infusionsoft that I, in fact, won the grand prize, it was finally time for me to experience my Celebratory Moment. The awards night was going to be held during Infusionsoft's annual conference for partners, PartnerCon, a couple of months after the contest ended.

With my packed bags in hand, I walked out the front door of my home to find the limousine Infusionsoft had sent so I could arrive in style at the conference. I could hardly contain my excitement as I embarked on my way to celebrate in the Winner's Circle. My first stop was to pick up my husband from work so we could head out for a lunch date together. Dining at one of our favorite restaurants, we spent our time reminiscing about the entire contest. We talked about the ups and the downs during this wild ride we had just experienced. Joe and I toasted to our victory and the anticipation continued to build toward my upcoming recognition — the Celebratory Moment— when I would finally receive the keys to my brand-new Chevy Camaro.

After lunch, we brought Joe back to work and the limo driver proceeded to head to the beautiful FireSky, a resort in Scottsdale, Arizona, where the conference was being held. It was the same venue where the ceremony was held the previous year. During the ride, I took some time to reflect back on the contest. I let the pride set in as I thought about the moment I declared the car was mine and how I was able to retrain my brain. I felt gratitude for the wonderful team who supported me, the many new clients I acquired, and the successful results they now saw in their businesses.

As we neared the resort entrance, a glimpse of the fabulous symbol of my victory caught my eye. The beautiful Camaro was parked right in front of the hotel entrance. A photographer greeted me and secretly snapped a few photos as I stepped out of the limo and saw the car for the first time. MY car, just as I had declared. There it was, right in front of my eyes! It was all shiny, beautiful, and RED! I touched it almost as if I had to check if it was for real! I had to contain the excitement because the big reveal wouldn't be until the next day during the awards dinner.

My friend, Jessica, who had been one of my biggest cheerleaders throughout the entire contest, met me out front. I had one more stop to make. Jessica and I rode around town in the limo, and I took her to one of my favorite little French bistros for a cocktail and a mini-celebration. Then we walked over to one of my favorite stores, because there was one more detail I needed to add to the visualization of my acceptance speech: the perfect necklace. I found it! It was big and bold and sure to add some dazzle to my outfit. Jessica and I headed back to the resort where we were welcomed by many of our colleagues who had arrived that night.

The next day I found it really hard to concentrate. During every meeting and keynote speaker, all I could really think about was how close I was to sharing my Celebratory Moment with my friends and family.

A few hours later, the time for the awards ceremony and dinner finally began! My husband, Joe, took my hand and told me how proud he was of me. Our two little girls twirled around in their sparkly dresses that we had picked out during our mother-daughter shopping trip the week before. Our son also looked very handsome. The kids sipped on kiddie cocktails. My parents and mother-in-law were also there, and together, we sat in the lounge before we headed inside the ballroom for the event. I was so proud to have my family there so they could share this moment with me, too.

It was the most perfect fall evening in Arizona, and many of my friends and colleagues were sporting their cowboy hats and boots because it was a Western-themed party. I, however, dressed for success that night—wearing my black dress that I had been visualizing, with my new purple shoes and my shiny new necklace to match. Joe and I enjoyed some cocktails on the terrace while laughing and joking with our friends—the other partners who had come from all over the world for the conference to learn, grow, and level up in their businesses. My photographer, Darby, was there to capture the special moments of the night.

Finally, it was time for dinner, and I began to live out the visualization I had imagined for so long. The banquet room was decorated beautifully, which added new surprises and details to the images of my Celebratory Moment that I hadn't even thought about. It was a perfect setting. There were hay bales, cowboy boots, and sunflowers in the table centerpieces. We sat down at our table and enjoyed our cowboy barbecue dinner.

The awards ceremony began and the announcements of third place and second place winners were a blur to me. Then, I heard those glorious words, "…and in first place, the grand prize winner of the Big Drive 2013, Janette Gleason!" To my surprise, my theme song, Rascal Flatt's "Red Camaro" began to fill the room. Some people in the crowd rose to their feet, applauding, cheering and whistling. I felt their love and support that night. My husband stood up and tipped me back for a kiss while our youngest daughter, Jillian, hugged me tightly. I headed up the steps onto the stage and, to my great delight, was handed a trophy—my very first "1st place" trophy! I squealed and hugged Brian, the announcer. People snapped pictures and Brian said, "Did anyone see that amazing car out front? That beautiful red Camaro? Well, it's my pleasure, Janette, to hand you the keys to your brand-new car." I held the keys up over my head in celebration of my victory, just like the race car champion would do with that cup.

I asked for my few moments to say my acceptance speech, and it was just as I had imagined it would be—except this time, I clearly saw the faces in the crowd and felt the love, pride, and gratitude magnified. I brought my husband and kids up on stage and got to watch them enjoy the spotlight. Jillian was quite the ham. She loved making the audience laugh with her silly faces and her Vanna White moves. Our other two children, Joey and Jianna, held their chins up with pride and smiled at being up on the stage with their mother. For me, my dream had finally come true.

I received so many hugs and kind words of congratulations, and after saying our "goodbyes," it was time to sit in my new car for the first time. I drove my beautiful car with my husband at my side and my kiddos in the backseat. They laughed and squealed as we went around the block in our sporty new ride!

One of my greatest accomplishments from this entire experience was showing my children that you can do anything you set your mind to. It overwhelms me with emotion whenever I think about that. To this day, I drive the car with pride, even when I received my first speeding ticket! I have so many other mementos that I carry with me from that night. I have wonderful pictures. I even find a little tiny speck of glitter in the Camaro every now and then, from the dresses our girls wore that night. It really was a truly magical and transformative experience.

YOUR TURN IN THE WINNER'S CIRCLE

It's been my privilege to be able to share in the Celebratory Moments with some of my clients. As a coach, I've had the honor of witnessing my clients, overwhelmed with joy, as they receive their prize, congratulate their team, sink their toes in the sand, and more. For me, part of that honor is being able to celebrate and enjoy their achievements with them.

I joined an executive team for their Celebratory Moment, a dinner where we reminisced about the experience. That night was a magical night. After our special dinner and toast to the success of the team, we gathered outside around a fire pit. All of the team members had brought their Achieve Boxes with them to the event, and it was time to open them up and read the statements that had been written inside. One by one each person read an "I Believe" or "I Am"statement to the group and tossed it into the fire. One of the team members, Geoff, explained to me "how amazing it was to spend that time celebrating together. That social moment when we sent off our goals into the sky." Another team member, Chris, told me, "The Celebratory Moment was one of the most important moments in my life. When we read our statements, and saw that they had all come to fruition, it was magical."

You too, can make the most of your Celebratory Moment by doing the following:

- **Enjoy every moment.** It's your special day. Allow yourself to bask in the glory of your accomplishments! Take the time to stand back and be pleased with what you've created.

- **Document the event.** Capture the moments of the day or event with pictures or videos. Have someone take photographs or videos for you. They'll help you remember the special details that occurred throughout your red letter day.

- **Gather mementos.** Throughout your Celebratory Moment, look for souvenirs to keep as reminders of your success: the program from the awards ceremony, a seashell from the beach, an extra party favor, or your trophy. Gather these keepsakes to serve as reminders of that moment when you realized your dream.

- **Share the moment with others.** Allow others to share in your joy. Surround yourself with the special people in your life. Whether it's your family, friends, co-workers, or team members, share your moment with them. Reminisce about your journey to success and encourage them to go after their dreams, too.

- **Express gratitude.** Throughout your Celebratory Moment, feel and express your gratitude. With your words or tokens of appreciation, thank the people around you and acknowledge the help they gave you along the way.

WHAT'S NEXT?

You've had the pleasure of celebrating and enjoying your Celebratory Moment. When it's done you might be asking yourself, "Okay, what's next? The party is over. Now what do I do?" Don't worry if you don't have the answer quite yet. There are some things you can do in the meantime:

1. **Assemble new tokens of success.** After The Big Drive awards ceremony, I took all of the fabulous photos from the event and created a beautiful album. I also carry a photo from that night in my wallet. It was one that my mentor, Trish, snapped of me kissing my son on the head right before I headed up on stage. Every time I open my wallet, I see that picture. It makes me feel incredibly strong, proud and grateful. Also, we still have the giant magnets that Infusionsoft made for the sides of the car, with my picture and the words "Congratulations, Janette Gleason, Winner of The Big Drive." My husband put them on the fridge in our garage, and every time I grab a bottle of water, I look at those magnets, smile and think, "Wow, that was so much fun!" The greatest token of all is the Camaro itself. Each time I drive it, I feel gratitude. I make a point to put my hand on the dashboard and say, "thank you." Gratitude and a sense of accomplishment overcome me whenever I get into my car.

   How can you display your new tokens and reminders of your Celebratory Moment? Here are some ideas:

   - Create a framed picture collage from the event or from your journey.
   - Arrange your mementos on a shelf, a mantle, or a piece of furniture.
   - Put together a scrapbook or photo album.
   - Create a shadow box.
   - Frame your certificate, diploma, or acknowledgement.

Enjoy this process and involve others if you need some help. Remember, earlier in the book I talked about creating a support system where you figure out the areas in which you need assistance and find people to fill those gaps? This might come into play here as well. You might have a friend who is very crafty or creative, reach out to that person for ideas.

2. **Keep records of the encouraging messages that you receive.** After The Big Drive, I created "feel good" folders, a physical folder for handwritten cards and notes, and one on my laptop for electronic messages and posts on social media. As the warm and heartfelt messages started flowing in, congratulating me on my big win, I placed them in my folders. Anytime I need a pick-me-up or want to go after something big, I read them, and they make me feel so empowered. I invited my client, Brian, to do the same when he achieved his goal of getting a new job in a high-level leadership position. As he made the transition to his new role, he received a flood of positive comments and well wishes for his new endeavor. Brian kept record of each and every one and later said how important this was for him during the transition. He told me, "These will carry me through any fear or uncertainty about the next phase for me, now and in the future."

What are you waiting for? Create a folder or box for the encouraging words you receive. The next time you go after another big, hairy, audacious goal or you hit some obstacles along the road, read them to help you get back to a state of belief.

3. **Prepare for a potential crash.** After I drove home from the conference and got settled back into my normal routine again, I experienced a catharsis (a breaking down of the old) and a flood of emotions released. I cried. I sobbed. I slept for hours from pure exhaustion. I felt afraid at times. How would I live up to this level of success? I thought, "Is this it?" What could top this amazing experience? Had I reached a peak I could never rise above again? I allowed myself to just let it all out. I began to think about what was next for me and found myself patiently waiting for that answer.

Be aware of this potential crash you may also experience when your Celebratory Moment has come and gone. After this really exhilarating ride and the momentum you had built, you will eventually get back to your normal life. When this happens, you might experience a variety of emotions. You may become overwhelmed with sadness, loneliness, or boredom. You may even experience a bout of mild depression or fear. Just be aware of it. Remember it's a breaking down of the old and a building up of the new you. Allow yourself to go through it and apply some of these suggestions:

- Engage in a fun or entertaining activity.
- Talk it through with a close friend or family member.
- Express yourself creatively by writing, painting, or singing.
- Pray or meditate.
- Read the encouraging messages in your "feel good" folders.
- Look at your photos and mementos from your Celebratory Moment.
- Seek help and counsel, if needed.

4. **Take a break.** After your victory celebration, you will want to make time to fill the well by relaxing and resting. Make time for sleep. Take care of yourself by doing something that you love. Maybe it's spending time with family, getting a massage, playing a game, or reading a book. During this period of rest, it's a great time for you to reflect on your journey to the finish line. What did you learn during your experience? What did you do that contributed to your success? What mistakes did you make? What are the things that you learned about yourself? As you reflect, try journaling or talking to others about your thoughts and insights.

Ease your way back into a normal routine. My client, Lisa, had thoughtfully planned ahead for her Celebratory Moment as she set out to become Infusionsoft's Small Business ICON in 2014. She planned a tropical vacation with her husband after the conference. This was a great way for them to decompress after a long, exhausting journey. You may not be able to plan a long getaway, but you could certainly rest up for a weekend or even a few hours before getting back to the daily grind. Take a break for as long as you need to get yourself ready for that next race or that next mountain to climb.

5. **Pay it forward.** After your success, it's your turn to encourage others to go after their goals, too. Begin to share your story. Consider writing a blog about your experience. Teach your friends, your team, and your family about what you've learned and share your tools and strategies. When you come across individuals who express a desire to achieve something big, tell them you can't wait to see their success, visit their new house, read their new book, or buy their new product.

   You can also pay it forward by becoming a mentor or coach. Just as you seek help from coaches and mentors, you can give back, one person at a time. Is there someone heading down a similar path that you just finished? Maybe you could shorten his or her learning curve and make the process easier. If you've just crushed your revenue numbers, maybe you could give a workshop on how you did that and give some tools and strategies to others. If you won a contest, maybe take one of next year's finalists under your wing and help that person know what that experience is going to be like and how they can be successful, too. If you bought the home of your dreams, encourage another to do the same. Be that mentor, take the time to help somebody else achieve something big.

6. **Start anew.** Now that you've achieved your goals and you've had some time to rejuvenate, you'll be thinking about when to start again. You'll start asking yourself, "What's the next experience I want to create? Am I ready to climb another giant mountain or do I still just want to take some time to rest and relax? Do I have a big goal or a small goal?" When you have a desire to achieve more, I encourage you to go back to the beginning of this book. It will be time for you to

look at your bucket list and review the top 100+ things you want to be, do, or have. Start crossing off things that you've accomplished. Begin to dream again. When the next fire is lit inside of you, you'll be ready to get in the race again and continue forward to your next finish line.

DISCOVERING YOUR TRUE PURPOSE

Earlier this year, I attended a charity breakfast with Kim Kiyosaki from the company, Rich Dad, Poor Dad. Kim was giving a talk about the "law of precession," and her words really moved me because they brought everything full circle for me regarding achieving my goals.

The law of precession is taught by Buckminster Fuller, and it simply says, "For every action we take, there will be a side effect arising at 90 degrees to the line of our action." What does this mean? Let's take, for example, a pebble dropping into a body of water. Once that pebble hits the surface, the water will ripple out away from it at a 90-degree angle. This can have some great side effects. These ripples might be carrying sea creatures to where they need to go. They could form a wave that ends up on the seashore.

Another example that Kim shared was about the honeybee. The bees spend their lives going from flower to flower. They think that their purpose is to collect the nectar and make honey. But what is the effect that's happening at a 90-degree angle from that action? The greater impact is pollination. When the honeybee gets nectar at the flower, pollen gets on the bee. The bee carries the pollen to another flower and pollination occurs. The bee's goal of getting the honey has a bigger purpose, and that is for pollination: the wondrous process that grows gardens, creates beautiful meadows of flowers, and so much more.

Kim's thoughts began to make me think about my goals and how they can impact the world in a much bigger way. Just as the honeybee thinks its goal is to collect nectar to make honey, during The Big Drive, it was my goal to win the contest and bring home the Camaro. Since earning the grand prize, I have reflected on the effects that occurred at a 90-degree angle from my victory. I've asked myself, "Who did I become?" Not only am I now a first place winner, but I also discovered in me a driven salesperson, a team leader, and a stronger, more driven businesswoman. My true purpose, those side effects, have been unveiling over time as I share my experiences with people I meet. I talk about how I made the declaration of bringing home that Camaro. I share how I automated those email messages that helped me stay positive. I explain to people how I visualized my Celebratory Moment. As a result, I'm coaching others to reach for the nearly impossible and to achieve their wildest dreams. It has been my true privilege to experience others achieving their goals and watching them succeed. As my clients plant the seeds of their desires, I get to help them tend the soil, pull the weeds, and watch them grow into beautiful gardens, just as our friends, the honeybees, do.

Yes, the car is fun to drive, and I enjoy remembering the road to my sweet success, but the true reward has actually been in the impact my experience has had on others—especially you, my beloved reader. I've discovered that the true purpose of me winning the Camaro is to inspire, uplift, and empower others to achieve their goals as well.

"What you get by achieving your goals is not as important as what you become by achieving your goals."

~ Henry David Thoreau

Now it's your turn to write the end of your story as you cross the finish line, experience a transformation, and take your turn in the Winner's Circle.

After you achieve your goals, take some time to reflect and describe the new you. Identify those effects occurring at a 90-degree angle from the achievement of your goals. What is your true purpose? What was the purpose of you achieving those goals? You're going to see those ripple effects of the people that you've helped or will help and the transformation that's occurred within you.

It is my wish that you not only succeed in your endeavors but that you absolutely crush your goals. My hope is that you give it your all as you cross that finish line and celebrate all of your life's victories. I wish that you live the life of your dreams, enjoy the ride to your greatest achievements, and discover your true purpose along the road to your sweet success. Thank you for being "you," for going after your goals, and for allowing me to join you on this ride. Wishing you infinite amounts of success and wishing ALL your dreams come true!

 GET INTO GEAR

- Enjoy your Celebratory Moment and your turn in the Winner's Circle.

- Share the experience with others and express your gratitude.

- Gather your mementos and tokens of success.

- Experience your transformation and then allow yourself to take a break.

- Pay it forward.

- Understand how the "law of precession" applies to your actions.

- Reflect on what the true reward is from achieving your goal.

- Describe the new you, including the impact you have made on others.

ACCELERATE TOWARD YOUR SUCCESS

1. Plan how you will document the day. I cannot stress enough how important it is to do this. You will be so busy enjoying your achievement, that taking photos or recording video over the course of the day will be the last thing on your mind. However, capturing these special moments are tangible ways you can relive your success. Whether you hire a photographer and videographer or ask a family friend to fulfill this role, just remember to delegate this important task.

2. Start anew by beginning to think about what's next. You have been working hard to achieve your goals and deserve to take time for rest and relaxation. As you refuel your mind and rejuvenate your spirit, start

thinking about what's in store for you now. This is the perfect time to reflect on your true purpose. Can you mentor others who want to follow in your footsteps? Do you want to write about your experience and share it with the masses? Take this time to find your true heart's desire before you start on your road to sweeter success.

ON THE ROAD REFLECTIONS

While pursuing your dreams and achieving your goals, you will become a transformed person. How can you give back and share your experience with others? Will you become a mentor, coach others, or write a blog article? Think about how you can make a difference and write about it in your journal.

**Enjoy every second of your Celebratory Moment.
Reflect on your experience, feel the appreciation,
and enjoy the success you've created.**

The FAST TRACK
to Success

> "It's not just about achieving your goal, it's also about who you become by achieving it."
>
> ~ Janette Gleason

You've just read about my 10 principles to success. You've gone through the activities to identify your goals, visualize your Celebratory Moment, and take action each day. And, I hope you've been inspired by my journey on the road to sweet success.

While you might be revving your engine and ready to go, you also might feel uncertain about the course. I've been so blessed to have this chance to write my story, to share my experience in the driver's seat. Now, I'm taking on the new role of pit crew chief, and I'm enjoying every minute of it. I have come to learn that we don't create alone. We all need a hand in achieving our goals. If you want to achieve sweet success the way I have, hire me! I can help you get to the Winner's Circle. With my programs and services as your map, you'll be headed in the right direction, moving closer to that checkered flag.

My programs and services are designed to help you:

- Aspire by providing direction as you identify your hopes and ambitions

- Activate by helping you get started in the right direction toward achieving your goals

- Accelerate by assisting you in moving toward your goals faster than you thought

- Adapt by pointing out how to change your behavior in order to better set yourself up for success

- Achieve by motivating you to accomplish everything you ever dreamed possible and more

- Ascend by completing your transformation as you move into the role of influencer and mentor

If you would like to continue your journey to success with me and other See It, Achieve It ™ coaches, please visit www.janettegleason.com to learn more about how our programs can benefit you.

SEE IT, ACHIEVE IT™ PROGRAMS AND SERVICES

Achieve Circles™: These small groups are designed to be a support system as you work toward accomplishing your goals. Receive guided instruction, learn tools and strategies, and engage in activities that will help you succeed. These regular meetings provide opportunities to network and seek advice on your goal-achievement progress. As part of a Circle, you'll also receive access to a private online forum and a resource binder filled with worksheets and action items.

Private Coaching: Whether you are an executive or leader at a multimillion-dollar company or a small business owner, I will guide you in becoming more focused with your goals during these sessions. Together, we will work on developing a mindset that is honed in on success, eliminating obstacles, and taking the right kind of action that leads you closer to your goals every day. These sessions can be offered in person, by phone, or a combination of both.

VIP Day: We'll spend the day focusing on your project at hand. Whether you need me to consult on your automated marketing campaigns, develop a strategic plan for your business, or create an action plan for achieving your goals, you will have my undivided attention as we collaborate on this important task.

Live Virtual Training and Coaching: With a variety of virtual opportunities at your fingertips including webinars, group coaching, book clubs and more, you'll enhance your knowledge and gain insights that will help you take your life and business to the next level.

Motivational Speaking: As a best-selling author with a compelling story to tell and proven strategies to share, I am available for keynote and breakout sessions designed to motivate audiences to take action. Presentation topics include talking about learning from failures, my personal transformation, and my 10 Success Principles.

Creative Workshops: I offer a number of workshops that can be conducted for small groups to entire departments or companies. All of these workshops have one result in mind: helping you and your team achieve goals. My workshops include helping participants create Achieve Boxes or design Focus Boards. I also moderate goal-setting sessions.

Corporate Leadership Coaching: If you would like me to work with your team, we can create a customized course of activities that include a variety of my services and programs. Your coaching package can include Achieve Circles, private coaching, access to self-study courses, and monthly Q & A or update calls to ensure everyone is moving forward to help the company succeed.

Products and Self-Study Programs: For those who have the discipline of working toward their goals on their own, I offer self-study programs including an online course, Achieve, a set of 10 classes that served as the foundation for *The Road to Sweet Success*. A supplement to this online course is the resource binder that we use to guide our Achieve Circle meetings. I also offer Achieve Box kits and am in the process of developing exciting, new products including action item card decks, CD sets, and a line of journals.

See It, Achieve It ™ Training and Certification Program for Coaches: Become a certified See It, Achieve It ™ Coach and help others transform their lives by guiding them to achieve their own big, hairy, audacious goals. Receive training to lead your clients through my 10 Success Principles.

To learn more about my programs, services, and products, please visit my website at www.janettegleason.com or contact me at janette@janettegleason.com.

More Client Testimonials

**"What makes a good coach?
Complete dedication."**

~ George Halas

"Through Janette's personal mentoring, in-person meetings, and workshops with my team, I was able to achieve and maintain a state of belief about accomplishing three lofty goals we set for our department in Q4. Janette empowered the team to not only hit our year-end goals but exceed them, too! Her mastery of continuing to believe in periods of doubt is world class. What a great way to end the year!"

~ **Elizabeth Pitt**, Chief Customer Officer, Infusionsoft

"When we decided to enter the Infusionsoft Small Business ICON competition in 2014, Janette encouraged us to go for it and helped us believe we could win. She shared some key strategies that gave us the confidence to enter with a winning attitude. For all the support and guidance she gave us up to and including winning the grand prize, we will be forever grateful."

~ **Lisa & Hamish Macqueen**, Owners, Cleancorp

"In the pursuit of performance and goals, many of us get in our own way. Janette has an incredible gift of being able to help you clearly articulate what you want and why you want it without having the how hold you back. Her daily positive focus and coaching helped me exceed my goals faster than I believed possible. She practices what she preaches. She generously shares how champions are made through her own firsthand experience. If you listen closely, she'll help you unlock the door to unlimited success."

~ **Brian Jambor**, Director of Partner Marketing, Yodle

"Janette Gleason's online course, Achieve, is the key to unlocking your successful future! She cares deeply for her clients and believes in them as they reach their goals! I'm blessed to have her in my life, and recommend you reach out to her when you are ready to ACHIEVE!"

~ **Laura Clancy**, CEO and Founder, Muffin Toppled ™

"Janette's calm coaching style helped me focus on my next step and provided the support and accountability to help me reach my goals. By sharing her own success story, Janette was genuinely empathic and excited to help me succeed because she's been there and followed the action steps she coaches on. The combination of resources and activities provided, delivered in a very organized process, prompted me to take action and gave me the confidence and belief in myself to achieve my goals."

~ **Lara Endorf**, Infusionsoft Certified Partner, Solutions by Lara

"I'm sure I'm not the only one who's ever wandered in and out of goals. You know, "I think I'll learn Spanish" or "I'm going to hike Everest." It's not enough to hang out in the theoretical. Janette was able to help me really focus on the three things I'm willing to work on every day. I walked away from our first call together with as clear a picture as I've ever had about what I need to do next. More importantly, she listened and helped me identify a few things that have been standing in my way. She's the real deal."

~ **Thomas Jones**, Sr. Manager of Professional Services, Infusionsoft

"Janette's Mompreneur Mindset group coaching course is a MUST for all mom's trying to build a business while managing a crazy, hectic life at the same time. She has provided me invaluable, excellent tools to help me put my whole entire life in order and grow from there all while being fulfilled at the same time."

~ **Michele Carter**, Independent Distributor, Young Living

"Clarity and confidence. When I think of my time working with Janette, what stands out most to me is her ability to coach others to live and perform with the same focus and confidence that she possesses. Whatever Janette does, she does with excellence, whether it is as a mom, wife, business owner or friend, but she isn't content with simply succeeding herself: she wants to see others succeed as well. Through her Mompreneur coaching program, Janette spends time in both group sessions and one-on-one conversations, helping us to set goals and then, gain clarity and confidence around reaching those goals. My time with Janette has transformed the way I approach situations because she has given me the tools to assess, find solutions and then act with confidence.

Thank you, Janette, for sharing so generously with others what you have worked hard to cultivate in your own life. You are an amazing coach and mentor."

~ **Tracy Moore**, Infusionsoft Certified Partner

"Participating in Janette's Mompreneur Mindset group coaching program has been an incredible experience. Each week, she's shared her expertise and resources to help moms like her create a lifestyle that encourages a balance of family and career. I highly recommend this program to all moms because Janette's knowledge and success will inspire and prepare them to take their businesses to the next level or to take the leap into mompreneurship."

~ **Mary Ann Rausa**, MAR Communications Group

"I watched Janette for two years while she methodically moved her way through one award and goal after another. She did not know me as I was simply a person on her list that she would send out encouraging emails to along the way. Then I decided to engage with her at one of her in-person events [a strategic planning day]. I was fortunate to have some one-on-one time with her to scope out my BIG, HAIRY, AUDACIOUS GOALS, and that was the moment I learned that Janette sees everything as curriculum. By using her teacher training skill sets, she maps out a process or service just one time and then, it becomes a book, class, or course. This is her secret sauce, she knows how to zero in on a project and then, "voila" it is done. She is your teacher and guide, and she sets you up for success and helps you with tangible goals to ACHIEVE them."

~ **Robin Bramman**, COO, CodeRed-I.com
Founder, BrandHappyHour.com
Master Brand Strategist, RobinBramman.com

"I was searching for a mentor who could help me uncover work-life balance as a mom, business owner and spiritual seeker. Janette Gleason answered my prayers and more. She has a gift for turning chaos into order by systemizing all that is required to get immediate responsibilities done and move goals forward on a daily basis. I recommend Janette as a sure-fire mentor to anyone who is searching for heart-centered methods and strategies to push their career and personal development upward."

~ **Raven Kleinbach**, Infusionsoft Expert, Clever Automation

Acknowledgements

**"We must find time to stop and thank the people
who make a difference in our lives."**

~ John F. Kennedy

To my husband, business partner, and best friend, Joe Gleason -
Thank you for being my biggest fan and for teaching me how to dream big. I love you, always and forever.

To my family and friends –
Thank you all for your love, support, and encouragement. Your belief in me keeps me headed in the direction of my dreams.

To my crew chief, Mary Ann Rausa –
Thank for standing by my side every step of the way during this journey. You are a priceless gift to me, and I appreciate your talent, dedication, and support.

To my experts and technicians –
Thank you for helping me make my dream of writing this book a reality! Many thanks go to: Patricia DeSantis for transcribing my spoken word so I never have to start with a blank page; Candy and the iCandy Design team for taking what is in my mind and bringing it to life; Brandi Hollister for designing this beautiful book cover and interior layout; Darby Simon for your photography and always capturing just the right moment; Fawn Cheng and Rachel Gilbert for making me feel beautiful; Robin Bramman for your branding expertise, friendship and support; Bryan Illguth and June Brockmeyer for helping me look and sound good on camera; and Lynn Mathers for editing and adding the finishing touches to my book.

To my NASCAR consultant, Aaron Johnson –
Thanks for all your insight and knowledge into the world of racing. It's been so much fun learning about green flags, confetti cannons, kissing the bricks, and more!

To my Big Drive pit crew –

Thank you to my virtual assistants Martha Morones, Becky Xourafas, and Cori Sweetalla; my marketing automation coaches Tracy Moore and Liz Ullery; my copywriter Kerri Cassone; and my campaign strategist Melanie Pittman. Thank you for the hours and hours of work and dedication. I'm truly grateful.

To my Big Drive MVP, Cory Bendixen –

Thank you for your support and for pushing me to keep going, helping me gain confidence, picking me up when I was down, and for cheering me on until the very last moment of the race when I crossed the finish line!

To my teachers, mentors, and coaches: Pamela Slim, Sonia Choquette, and Trish McCarty –

Thank you for your continued wisdom, guidance, and support.

To Chuck Trautman and my fellow mastermind members –

I appreciate your advice, encouragement, and friendship throughout the years.

To my dear friend and client, Lisa Macqueen -

Thank you for allowing me to share in the joy of your achievements. I'm so glad we can connect even though we live on opposites sides of the Earth. You are a dear friend and a true example of success.

To Elizabeth Pitt –

Thank you for allowing me the honor to join your team of leaders and pass along the joy of the creative process to others. You inspire me to achieve more and to reach for my dreams.

To the Infusionsoft partner community –

You are an extraordinary group of people filled with brilliant minds with a passion for small business success. Thank you for your generous support, knowledge, and friendship.

To the executive team and staff at Infusionsoft –

To the executive team and staff at Infusionsoft – Thank you for building an amazing software program dedicated to helping small businesses succeed. I'm grateful for the doors you have opened for me to grow personally and professionally while fulfilling my purpose. My hope is that this book will convey to you the impact you have had on my life and how much I appreciate you.

To my Achievers –
My greatest joy is watching you learn, grow, and crush your goals! I am honored to have the opportunity to join you on your road to sweet success.

About the Author

The **See It, Achieve It™** coach, Janette Gleason focuses on guiding individuals to realize their dreams. Through her courses, workshops, strategy sessions and keynote addresses, her expertise and counsel has helped many people, including small business owners as well as leaders and executives at multi-million dollar corporations reach the next level of success.

Since founding her company in 2011, Janette quickly developed a reputation as a professional who produces significant results. Her strong background and passion for database marketing led her to become an Infusionsoft Certified Consultant, a 2011 Ultimate Marketer Finalist and the 2013 grand prize winner of The Big Drive sales competition, which served as inspiration for this book.

Janette has appeared in numerous print and online publications, podcasts and television shows, including: *BusinessWeek*, *ExpertPreneur Magazine*, *Yahoo! Finance*, and *Forbes Magazine*, which named her a Game Changer. In addition, Janette received a Quilly Award from the National Academy of Best-Selling Authors, ranked among the top 10 on Startup Nation's Leading Moms in Business Competition, and was named a 2015 Arizona Mother of Achievement by American Mothers, Inc. Her book, *Transform*, co-written by Brian Tracy, a leading expert in personal and business development, is a best-seller on Amazon.

Janette is married with three beautiful children and lives in Surprise, Arizona.

To connect with Janette:

- Visit http://www.janettegleason.com
- Find her on Facebook at https://www.facebook.com/gleasonconsulting
- Connect with her on LinkedIn at https://www.linkedin.com/in/janettegleason
- Follow her on Twitter @janettegleason